Dramatic

Dramatic Science is an invaluable tool for any teachers and primary science leaders who have classes of 5–11-year-olds. It provides the busy professional with a range of tried and tested techniques to use drama as a support and aid to the teaching of science to young children.

The techniques within this book offer innovative and creative strategies for teaching a challenging area of the curriculum and broadening teachers' own scientific knowledge and understanding.

All the strategies in this book have been shown to work effectively in a range of primary schools. The approaches described offer an inclusive and participatory way to teach science and the authors provide a pedagogical commentary on the ways that teachers have tried and tested the techniques and how they have worked best. Reflective discussion on the strategies will include discussion about how the children have responded to these strategies and how the drama experiences have impacted on their learning.

This invaluable resource:

- supports working and thinking scientifically;
- develops critical and creative thinking;
- scaffolds creative learning;
- broadens teachers' scientific knowledge and understanding;
- enhances children's understanding of science;
- provides guidance on active and participatory learning;
- can engage children and teachers at a variety of levels;
- links science to real life;
- heightens children's application of science to different situations;
- develops problem solving and enquiry skills; and
- enhances and extends speaking and listening skills.

Any teachers wishing to hone their practice to motivate children and improve their science learning and attainment will find this an invaluable resource. It will also be useful for science leaders, specialist teachers and other professionals who are involved in supporting schools to improve the quality of learning in science and other subjects, trainee teachers and NQTs interested in developing creative learning in their classrooms.

Prof Debra McGregor works in the School of Education at Oxford Brookes University. She has worked within primary, secondary and tertiary education, in both the USA and the UK. She has been involved in producing innovative curriculum materials as well as researching and writing about teaching and learning processes.

Dr. Wendy Precious works across the West Midlands as a Primary Science Education Consultant for Entrust (formerly Staffordshire LA). She is also a tutor for the Science Learning Centre, and a Hub Leader and Assessor for the Primary Quality Mark. She has developed effective and creative teaching resources, and coaches and mentors education professionals to reflect on and improve science learning within the classroom, the whole school and the local community.

Dramatic Science

Inspired ideas for teaching science
using drama ages 5–11

Debra McGregor and
Wendy Precious

 Routledge
Taylor & Francis Group

NEW YORK AND LONDON

First published 2015
by Routledge
2 Park Square, Milton Park, Abingdon, Oxon OX14 4RN

and by Routledge
711 Third Avenue, New York, NY 10017

Routledge is an imprint of the Taylor & Francis Group, an informa business

© 2015 Debra McGregor and Wendy Precious

British Library Cataloguing in Publication Data
A catalogue record for this book is available from the British Library

Library of Congress Cataloging-in-Publication Data

McGregor, Debra.
Dramatic science : inspired ideas for teaching science using drama, ages 5–11 / Debra McGregor and
Wendy Precious.
pages cm
1. Science—Study and teaching (Primary)—Activity programs. 2. Drama in education—Study and
teaching (Primary)—Activity programs. I. Precious, Wendy. II. Title.
LB1532.M35 2014
372.35′044—dc23
2014012421

ISBN: 978–0–415–53675–2 (hbk)
ISBN: 978–0–415–53677–6 (pbk)
ISBN: 978–0–203–11119–2 (ebk)

Typeset in Bembo
by Swales & Willis Ltd, Exeter, Devon

MIX
Paper from
responsible sources
FSC
www.fsc.org   FSC® C013056

Printed and bound in Great Britain by
TJ International Ltd, Padstow, Cornwall

Contents

List of appendices
Narratives to introduce scientists for KS1 or KS2

List of figures and tables

Figures

Tables

Foreword

Primary science needs innovative projects that work with teachers and children to create evidence-based outcomes from rigorous trials in schools. *Dramatic Science* offers exactly that and more.

I have been privileged to observe dramatic science in action and watched how this non-traditional approach to science both challenged and excited teachers, which led to changes in the way they approached the teaching of science. The material in this book is the product of a creative collaboration across different groups of people, blending expertise in science and drama with rigorous trialling in schools with teachers and children.

Dramatic Science explores and explains various drama techniques that involve children in considering science from different perspectives, including scientists themselves, bringing a human dimension to children's understanding of science. This approach is more than just fun and motivating, it is one that appeals inclusively to all children and develops their curiosity and confidence in acting and talking about science. Importantly this fusion of science and drama really helps children to develop a depth of understanding of key science concepts and of ways of working and thinking scientifically that they will remember long after the lesson.

This is a book that will change the nature of teaching and learning in primary science because it is based on evidence from the classroom: of what works, why it works and how to approach science. *Dramatic Science* illuminates children's thinking and engages them in memorable science experiences; read, enjoy and be prepared to be surprised.

Rosemary Feasey
Primary Science Consultant and former
Chair of Association of Science Education

Acknowledgements

This book has emerged from a series of collaborative projects carried out with primary teachers from Staffordshire and the West Midlands. The drama ideas grew from professional development work originally carried out by McGregor and Precious (2010) with teachers in the Stafford area. The clarification and more rigorous testing of the innovative approaches emerged from working on projects funded by the AstraZeneca Science Teaching Trust (AZSTT, more recently re-launched as the Primary Science Teaching Trust (PSTT)). Some of the activities described in this book can be seen 'in-action' within the PSTT Continuing Professional Development Unit entitled 'Dramatic Science' (see http://www.pstt.org.uk/ext/cpd/dramatic-science).

Much appreciation is extended to Jill Rezzano for translating the authors' ideas and suggestions about the scientists and their lives and work to produce the drafted monologues.

Personal gratitude is also extended to the authors' families, who have been extremely patient whilst this project has come to fruition. The authors would like them to know that spending evenings and weekends collating and crafting this book was not an endeavour undertaken in preference to spending time with them, rather a determination to share and disseminate creative and innovative ideas to inform and develop primary science teaching.

Participants in the project

The projects involved a creative team and three development teams. The creative team was lead by Debra McGregor, a teacher educator and researcher, previously at the University of Wolverhampton and now at Oxford Brookes University. The other key members of the creative team were Wendy Precious, formerly the Primary Science Advisor for Staffordshire Local Authority and now an education consultant for Entrust, and Jill Rezzano, who is the Education Officer from the New Victoria Theatre in Newcastle-Under-Lyme.

The development teams (who tried, tested and refined the approaches) involved teachers from a range of schools in Staffordshire and the West Midlands as listed below:

- Barnfields Primary School, Stafford, Staffordshire
- Berkswich CE (VC) Primary School, Stafford, Staffordshire
- Dove Bank Primary School, Kidsgrove, Staffordshire
- Eton Park Junior School, Burton-on-Trent, Staffordshire
- Fredrick Bird Primary School, Coventry, West Midlands
- Gorsemoor Primary School, Cannock, Staffordshire
- Grange Infants School, Burton-on-Trent, Staffordshire
- Knypersley First School, Biddulph, Staffordshire
- Rounds Green Primary School, Sandwell, West Midlands
- St Augustine's CE (C) First School, Draycott-in-the-Clay, Staffordshire
- St John's CE (VC) Primary School, Keele, Staffordshire
- Gnosall St Lawrence CE (VC) Primary School, Staffordshire
- St Peter's CE (VA) Primary School, Caverswall, Staffordshire
- Thomas Russell Infants School, Barton-Under-Needwood, Staffordshire
- The Grove Primary School, Stafford, Staffordshire
- Wilnecote Junior School, Tamworth, Staffordshire

Reviewers

Thanks are also gratefully extended to Clarysly Deller (awarded PSTT Teacher of the Year 2013) and Mary Darby for carefully checking through the material in the book.

1

Introducing and defining dramatic science

The dramatic science approach can provide a lively, first hand opportunity for children to engage directly with scientific processes and concepts. There are varied opportunities to enact, explore, examine and question scientific ideas. Children, for example, could be asked to move like melting chocolate, create a 'frozen' moment in the germination of a seed or depict a skill they think Isaac Newton possessed as a young boy. The drama activities (in this book) are designed to encourage the development of curiosity and confidence in acting and talking about science in primary schools. They are intended to help to develop excitement and participation in learning. There are activities presented where the children are invited to improvise to represent a process or product, follow general guidance to demonstrate happenings or events or even recite from a script. For some strategies the children are required to mime; for others talk and discussion is vital. All the drama approaches, though, are designed to help to foster a sound understanding of, and about, science.

The approaches described in this book are designed to:

1. enable pupils to experience and observe phenomena;

2. allow pupils to look more closely at the natural and humanly-constructed world around them;

3. encourage pupils to be curious and ask questions about what they notice; and

4. help pupils to develop understanding of scientific ideas by using different types of scientific enquiry, such as:

■ answering their own questions;

■ observing changes over a period of time;

- noticing patterns;

- grouping and classifying things;

- carrying out simple comparative tests;

- finding things out using secondary sources of information;

- using simple scientific language to talk about what they have found out; and

- communicating their ideas in a variety of ways.

(Department for Education (DfE) 2013)

Overview (and intention) of the book

Each chapter in this book has been written with the reader very much in mind. Although we set out to provide very 'standardised' formats for each chapter, as the writing unfolded, the ways that our ideas were noted did not 'fit' a highly prescribed framework rigidly imposed to describe each drama convention. Some conventions are more straightforward and easy to describe (e.g. modelling in Chapter 7), others are much more complex (e.g. mini historical play in Chapter 9). Some approaches were also much easier for the teachers to (spontaneously) try out, for example, modelling and miming movement. Others required more preparatory work and planning, for example dressing up to engage in the monologues and mini historical plays.

Each drama convention, though, is introduced in a chapter, with explanations and illustrations about how it was intended to work. There are also photographs of the ways in which the strategies were used by the teachers, as well as some reflections and indications about the context in which they worked best. There is also discussion about the kinds of scientific skills and/or concepts the children appeared to develop or understand through engagement with particular drama strategies.

Towards the end of the book, there are suggestions about the different ways that the conventions can be utilised to deepen and broaden children's learning in science. Used in particular combinations, sequences or progression (see particularly Chapters 10 and 12) the different strategies can impact more intensely on the children's immersion in, and engagement with, the science activities.

This is not a complete account of all of our conventions, resources and ideas. It is, we hope, a rich description of some of the work-so-far that will prove useful for teachers to refer to and dip into for creative ideas about how to teach science.

Science and learning

Learning science is important for young children; as Harlen (2012) says, it is of value to them as individuals and of value for society.

Some of the different ways it can help children are briefly outlined below:

1. *Beginning to understand the real world* around them, to appreciate how things work (e.g. *How does electricity make lights come on?*; *How does heat change substances?*; or *How do trees grow?*). Alexander (2010: 149), asking children about their views of learning, found that they reiterated wanting to know 'how things work in the world', but that they also indicated they would like to know more about looking after animals and growing fruit and vegetables. These are the kinds of 'knowing about science' topics covered through the drama activities in this book. This aspect of learning in science can help to develop scientific literacy and lay foundations for grasping key concepts in science.

2. *Understanding scientific aspects of everyday life* that help inform the making of good personal choices about healthy living (e.g. *What type of food helps growth and repairs of the body?; What kind of exercise, and how much, is needed to stay fit and healthy?; How much water should we drink each day?*) and about caring for the environment. Being 'green' and contributing to sustainability for the planet (e.g. knowing what kind of rubbish, such as paper cups or plastic plates, can be recycled and how things, such as waste food, can be reused; knowing that leaving heating or lighting on when not needed is wasteful). This kind of scientific appreciation helps to develop better scientific citizenship.

3. *Engaging in scientific activities and enquiries* that offer the chance to *act* and *think* like a scientist can support learning science. Projects such as growing vegetables in the school grounds, caring for pets or surveying year six opinions on school lunches can provide suitable learning opportunities. These kinds of activities can aid comprehension of, and support understanding about, how to *think scientifically* and *work scientifically*.

    a. *Thinking scientifically* can include:

        i.   being able to answer challenging questions;

        ii. being able to ask good questions;

        iii. being able to see connections between things;

        iv. being able to discern trends or patterns in data;

        v.   being able to interpret and/or process information;

      vi. being able to use what you know to explain something new;

      vii. being able to devise a plan to investigate a question; and

      viii. being able to see flaws in arguments or ideas.

  b. *Working scientifically* can include:

      i. applying instructions to make something work;

      ii. carrying out an experimental plan;

      iii. being able to measure accurately using different equipment;

      iv. recognising how what you did influenced what you found out;

      v. being able to make reasoned judgements about the quality and reliability of data collected in experiments; and

      vi. being confident about making conclusions when evidence is trustworthy.

Effective science teaching that promotes enquiry can pique pupils' interest and stimulate their curiosity to want to find out more (Ofsted 2013).

4. *Appreciating that scientific knowledge we benefit from today* has accumulated over a long period of time. Understanding how what we know and can do scientifically and technologically has often resulted from personal human endeavours and persistence over time.

    All the above features can be brought to bear through appropriate use and development of the mini historical plays and scientists' short speeches (monologues). For example, after listening to a scientist's story, reflecting about what it means and applying that thinking to inform how to then investigate an idea connected to the scientist's discovery or invention re-quires all the above characteristics to be successful. See Chapter 9 for a more complete description of this.

The value of children *thinking* and *working scientifically*

Effective learning in science is needed because young children may intuitively think that magnets have a special glue, or are attracted to all metals. They may have overheard adults saying that plants need a *drink* because they are thirsty! Successful learning in science should help children to make observations, think about what they may see or hear, reflect and consider whether the new idea seems logical and 'fits with' or 'builds on' other understandings they already have. This is a constructivist approach to helping children learn, providing or scaf-folding learning experiences from which emerge, or are presented, phenomena to feel, see or hear (i.e. to *sense*) and be reflected upon. Consideration of new information, either through the questions that the teacher poses or that other children ask, helps to mediate and enhance meaning-making from the drama activities.

How drama supports constructivist learning in science

Drama can support constructivist learning because the children become active agents of their own learning. There are opportunities for them as individuals to communicate what they are thinking through varied modalities (Dorian 2009), explain their ideas to others, explore possible alternate views and opinions to build on and subsequently, as small groups, negotiate and agree collective thoughts.

Learning skills, therefore, that can be encouraged through drama, by working with classmates (to encourage social constructivism), include:

1. communicating clearly and effectively with each other;

2. sharing, explaining, negotiating and discussing ideas;

3. developing scientific literacy through clarifying each others' meanings and understandings;

4. collaboratively 'conveying' ideas through performing;

5. co-constructing simple solutions to problems; and

6. reflecting on what others 'mean' or 'think' (through dynamic and spontaneous discussion and interaction) as well as 'watching' other groups' recitals.

The DfE (2013) also indicate how teachers should have high expectations of their children and plan 'stretching work' for all of them. Drama provides an ideal approach to learning science that is inclusive, because much of the time the children can participate in their own personalised way to produce their own unique performance(s).

Outstanding learning in science – using drama

The Successful Science report (Ofsted 2011) describes an outstanding lesson as that which includes:

- reviewing previous work on minibeasts fieldwork in the school grounds, through paired discussion and then sharing with the whole class, to remind of the range of living things seen, and rekindle the sense of care needed to look after the environment;

- active watching of a butterfly video involving teacher questioning and children answering to agree the characteristics of living (and non-living) things;

- re-observing caterpillars to see how much they have grown to connect the key features of living organisms and the butterfly life cycle;

- the dressing up of a child in a cagoule (to represent the skin of the caterpillar) who is then enveloped in layers of toilet paper to represent the cocoon. The pupil illustrates breaking out of the layers with custom wings appearing from inside the cocoon; and

- the culminatory consolidation of the children instructing the teacher to re-enact development of caterpillar to butterfly.

There are many tried and tested ways, in this book, that dramatic strategies have been used to demonstrate scientific concepts similar to those described above.

Using drama to extend pedagogic repertoires

The drama strategies described in this book have been devised to help teachers to generate more exciting, creative and unforgettable learning experiences for their children. The approaches have emerged from working with teachers on various projects (McGregor 2010, 2011, 2012) and suggest ways in which the range of learning activities can be conceived, enhanced and extended for young people to more effectively learn science. Using drama is not about 'teaching to the test', nor should it be about delivering concepts in a safe, transmissive mode (Pollard et al. 2000; Reay & Wiliam 1999). It is intended to address the concerns of Alexander and Flutter (2009: 28), who claimed that 'Children and teachers are increasingly turned off science as it becomes a content-led, vocabulary-heavy subject where personal curiosity is thwarted and opportunities for children to develop investigative, questioning and thinking skills are limited'. Dramatic science has been established to provide both the teachers (and their classes) with a first-hand opportunity to engage directly with scientific processes and concepts, and to enact, explore, examine and question in various ways, ideas and theories in and about science.

Drama is, currently, a somewhat infrequently used teaching approach in science education, evidenced by the lack of curriculum materials and teacher support guides. Agogi and Stylianidou (2012), in their European review of practice, found that about 57 per cent of the teachers surveyed never or rarely used drama of any kind to teach early years science. This book, explaining the dramatic science project, has set about remedying not only the initiation of practice to use drama strategies to inform and develop science teaching, but has also endeavoured to describe these distinctive and stirring ways of helping teachers to engage children in learning a challenging subject through active and enjoyable experiences.

Although some of the eight strategies devised, developed and tested through the project had been applied previously for teaching, the majority of teachers indicated that they rarely used drama techniques to teach science (McGregor 2012), and some of them stated that they had never even thought of using such approaches to help the children to develop scientific understanding. The techniques they had used before were versions of hot seating, miming, storytelling, freeze frame and role play – but these were generally used to teach literacy or history and perform in assemblies.

Table 1.1 attempts to summarise the strategies that are further detailed throughout the book. Towards the end of the book the different strategies are 'connected' together to illustrate how they might be used in sequence to teach a particular topic or theme.

TABLE 1.1 List of drama conventions that were shown to support learning in science

Theatrical strategy	Application to support science learning
Mind movies	Can be used to 'transport' the learning to a different time or place, or to a particular event. It is an approach that can 'set the scene' for subsequent activities.
On-the-table	A class or small group are presented with an object (often unfamiliar). The object may be scrutinised from interesting angles with a magnifier or slowly revealed in intriguing ways.
Miming movement	Acting out ideas and thinking about how living things or objects work. Applies gestures and bodily actions. No speech involved (although groups can be given time to discuss and prepare to rehearse their enactment). This involves children in improvising to share their ideas.
Freeze frame	Freezing action (possibly as an aspect of miming movement, above) to create a still moment-in-time image. Usually managed by a tap on the shoulder or a clap of hands.
Modelling	This is often a still representation or demonstration of an organism or object, whereas miming movement is usually concerned with how an object/organism works.
Hot seating	Placing the teacher or children (who have particular expertise or experience) in the 'hot seat' to be questioned. The remainder of the class consider what they need to know and devise questions to ask of the character or expert-in-role.

TABLE 1.1 Continued

Theatrical strategy	Application to support science learning
Mini-historical plays	Teacher tells the group a story, which could be scripted, during which the children are guided to act out different events or actions of characters in the story.
Monologues (and related investigation, activity or experiment)	A mini-speech from a well-known scientist providing insights into their life and work. Carrying out a linked investigation, children are required to: think about their ideas and evidence; plan an experiment; systematically test ideas; obtain and present evidence; consider and make connections; solve practical problems; consider evidence; evaluate; and communicate these things to their peers and the teacher.

Teachers' reflections about using drama to help children to learn science

One teacher, who had already dabbled a little with drama, but was not conversant with all the conventions, said, 'What I've been impressed with is the emotive response [from the children] to science that it builds. You tend to think of science as something to do with concepts that is very cold. [It requires] . . . pro-formas of writing frequently, equipment, methodology, conclusion, hypothesis – [this is all] very dry and yet this [the drama] forces them to engage physically, mentally and emotionally with science and I think that's quite ground breaking' (year six teacher, West Midlands school). The idea 'that you can have fun and be creative in science rather than [just] analytical' was agreed widely among the participating teachers.

Another said, 'I think the whole structure of the course that you've [put together] is based on inquiry-based learning. When I was at school a book was put in front of you and you were told read Marianne North page forty-two and answer the questions at the end and you were really turned off. Whereas this, using drama, seeing the character come alive and you being encouraged to ask questions and learning that way, I think, is far more healthy, educationally wise' (year five teacher, West Midlands school).

Another teacher said, 'it's very inclusive, it helps children who find just accessing education through writing difficult'. She added that it also involves those who 'don't always put their hand-up in question and answer sessions, because they are physically involved in drama lessons'; 'From the comments the children make, they seem to really remember some of the things they have done through the drama'. She extends this to explain, 'the knowledge is reinforced through the drama, because they have used their bodies, talked about it and been involved in it' (year four/six teacher, North Staffordshire school).

CHAPTER

2

On the table

Introduction to the approach

This approach is designed to be a 'dramatic' introduction to an object or living organism. It works best if the 'object' is something that children are likely to be unfamiliar with, e.g. a pitcher plant (see Figure 2.1) or a 1930s tennis racket. Objects that they have not seen or come across before can effectively pique their interest. Seeing the extraordinary in the ordinary can be effective, too (e.g. magnifying different seeds and asking for predictions about how they may develop; slowly revealing inner parts of various fruits; or exploring the inside of a helmet and probing how they think it might be used and why). The approach is intended to be a strategy that hones children's observational skills as well as arousing their curiosity to 'want to find out more' and 'ask more questions'.

The approach can be developed in a number of ways:

1. *Hide and show*
   The teacher 'hides' the object or living organism (perhaps in a box with a black sheet over it, see Figure 2.1; 2.2) and moves the magnifier over interesting parts (whilst the whole thing is hidden) to show different and contrasting aspects. This could be presented as 'Guess what this is?', 'Why?' and 'How do you think it works?'

2. *Slow reveal*
   The teacher slowly reveals one part at a time (like the photographs suggest in Figure 2.3). This can be developed as 'What do you think this might be?' and 'Why?', showing only a small part initially, and as more of the object is revealed the questions might change to 'What do you think now?', 'Does seeing more change your view?', 'Why?'

3. *Close scrutiny*
   Closely observing a familiar object that is magnified presents a visual image that is not obvious, e.g. an orange, closely magnified, may present a bumpy

surface that is more reminiscent of the surface of a rocky planet or a gourd, which when magnified looks more like a loaf of bread (see Figure 2.3).

4. *What is it?*
    A student brings into school an unfamiliar object and 'shows' it to the rest of the class and they suggest from deductive observation what it might be (see Figures 2.3–2.7).

5. *What could it be?*
    This approach, using the 'feelie box' (Figure 2.5) draws on the sense of touch rather than 'looking' to work out what something might be from its physical features.

This strategy is intended to present what might be quite 'dramatic' visual images or partial features of an object that encourage children to carefully consider, scrutinise (and reconsider) what they are looking at, making detailed observations to infer (through responses to questions) information about the object.

The object can be slowly uncovered or hidden in a 'feelie box' and its features explored in a number of ways to intrigue the children.

Guidance to use 'on the table'

There are a number of ways in which this dramatic approach can be exploited (see the five different strategies outlined) to engage the children and focus their observations. The key objective is to 'present' an object, on the table (or desk), often 'hidden' (in a box or similar) for scrutiny by the senses (through touching or looking) that intrigues or grabs the children's attention because it is something unusual or it is magnified so it is viewed in an unusual way.

These objects can be an introduction to a topic, e.g. an unusual piece of sporting equipment or clothing to introduce 'sports' or an unfamiliar, but edible, plant to introduce 'food' or the inside workings of a torch to introduce 'electricity'.

1. *Hide and show*
    Usually this approach would be 'showing' from the front of the class using the white board (see http://www.azteachscience.co.uk/ext/cpd/dramatic-science/on-the-table.html), illustrated through the different images of Figure 2.1. Hiding an object from view in a box or under a black cloth can generate an air of mystery that can promote curiosity. The children can be openly asked to respond to each of the images, by saying, 'What can you see?', 'What do you think it is?', 'Why?' or they can each in turn be asked to prepare a statement that begins with the sentence stem 'I wonder if . . . because . . .'.

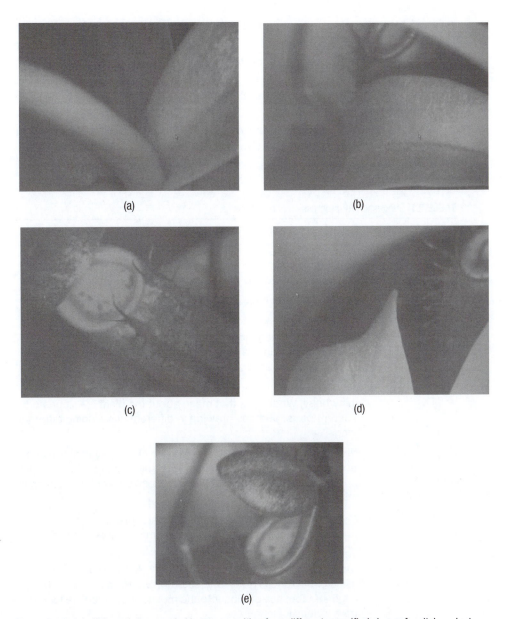

Figure 2.1 (a–e) Hide and show: varied images resulting from different magnified views of a pitcher plant

Figure 2.1a can be reflected upon to draw out how there may be a 'stem' and a 'leaf,' so it may be a plant of some kind.

Figure 2.1b shows that it isn't all the same colour green, that there are different textures and that it certainly doesn't appear to be a 'traditional' plant such as a daisy or daffodil!

Figure 2.1c shows an opening at the top of a long tube with a shiny rim at the top of it, and what looks like a lid that is hinged on the right! The plant has several of these hanging from the edge of the radiating leaves (see Figure 2.2).

Figure 2.1d indicates that the tube is long (it has water in the bottom to 'drown' small animals/insects).

Figure 2.1e shows how spiky or hairy the tube is and the contrast in texture and colour of the tubes and a leaf. The table below indicates how the questioning might progress to scaffold the children's thinking.

TABLE 2.1 Suggestion for progression of questions

Image (or figure referring to)	Question suggestions
2.1a	What can you see? [A: a tube-like stem and base (bottom) of a leaf, it's green and hairy]
	What kind of thing has a stem and a leaf? [A: a plant]
2.1b	How many colours are there? [A: 3 or 4] What colours? [A: pale green, darker green, bright green, purplish] What might the different colours indicate? [A: different parts to the plant/different parts of different ages]
	What kind of textures or surfaces can you see? [A: smooth/ shiny/hairy] What does that mean about the plant? [A: it has different parts, perhaps growing in different ways/doing different things]
2.1c	What does this part of the plant look like? [A: opening at top of a tube, shiny rim, hinged lid; hairs on lid; spikes on tube] Why might a plant have a tube with a lid that can close on it? [A: to trap small animals/insects]
	Why do you think it might have hairs and spikes? [A: to stop other bigger animals getting in to eat smaller ones trapped in tube]
2.1d	What else can you see from this picture? [A: the tube is long; inside of the tube is green and smooth; two rows of spikes the length of tube; spikes closer to the mouth of the tube are longer – more vicious looking!]
	Why might a plant like this have water in it? [A: to drown small creatures; to store water for dry times]
2.1e	How different is the tube to the leaf? [A: the leaf is smoother, greener; the top of the tube is shiny and ribbed] Why are these parts of the plant different, do you think? [A: tube – ribbed opening is stronger to hold it open to catch passing/thirsty small creatures].

2. *Slow reveal*

This approach can be adopted to purposely challenge the children's thinking. They may initially think that Figure 2.3a is a quarter of a sphere or a planet, perhaps. It is important, though, to ask them 'why' they think that. This promotes reflection on what they can see and encourages them to use what they already know to inform what they think something might be. Figure 2.3b may encourage responses that suggest it could be skin from an animal or a diseased person. Figure 2.3c might draw suggestions that it is a homemade loaf of bread or a large stone or rock. Figure 2.3e provides an image of the whole gourd (the dried shell of a part of a plant such as a cucumber or a pumpkin). Many children may not be familiar with gourds. It would be an interesting extension, within the topic of food, to magnify seeds and unusual foods from plants, and ask the children what they might grow into. Capsicum seeds or seeds from fruits can provide rich opportunities, not only to speculate about what food they will grow into (and what plant they come from), but also to predict what they may look like after germination and growth.

The children could also take turns in making a statement about each of the pictures, beginning with the sentence stem 'I wonder if . . .'. The teacher could then use the comments and observations (listed on a poster or white board) from the children to discuss the characteristics of the seeds or parts of plants further.

(a)

(b)

Figure 2.2 (a & b) A pitcher plant (aerial and side view)

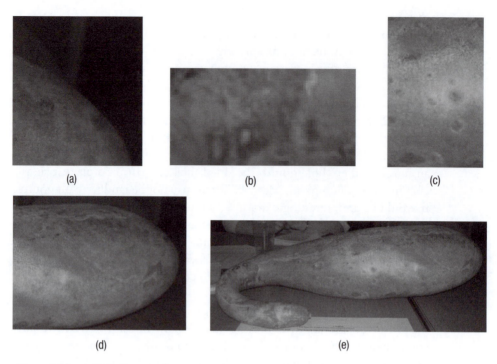

Figure 2.3 (a–e) Varied images resulting from different magnifications of a gourd

3. *Close scrutiny*

   Closely observing a familiar object that magnified presents a visual image that is not obvious, e.g. a pomegranate, closely magnified, may present a bumpy surface that is more reminiscent of the surface of a rocky planet or the inside of something that the students may often see from the outside (e.g. the inside of a torch or the inside of a clock).

4. *What is it?*

   The on–the–table approach can be used to explore any object that the children (or teacher) might bring in to school that the other students have not seen before, but the technique (illustrated in Figure 2.1; 2.3; 2.6) enables detailed and careful scrutiny so that plausible suggestions can be explored in a scientific manner. The kinds of questions that might be posed here could include:

   ■ What does it look like?

   ■ How can you describe it

   ■ Does it look similar to anything else you know?

   ■ Is it man–made or natural? Why do you think that?

   ■ What could it be? Why do you suggest this?

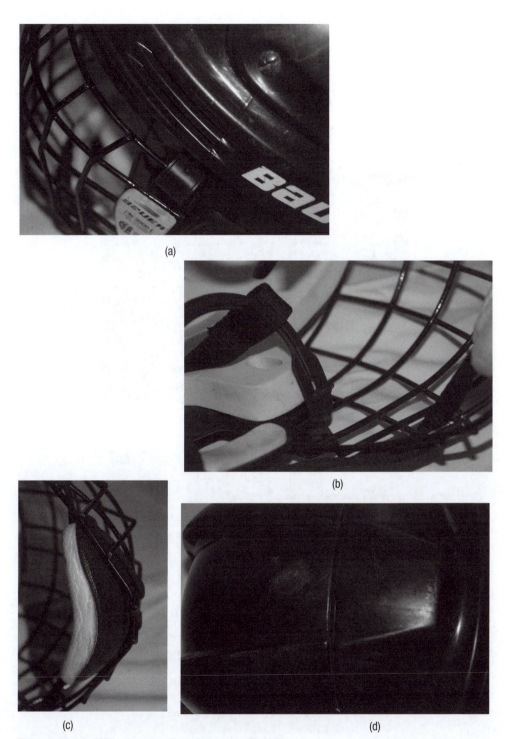

Figure 2.4 (a–d) Different perspectives of an ice hockey helmet

5. *What could it be?*

    This might be an object that the teacher or a child can identify (who then places it in the feelie box [Figure 2.5], or hides it under a cloth) and uses the magnifier to generate curiosity to closely observe and speculate about what the object might be (Figure 2.4; 2.7). The magnifier could be deliberately positioned to examine the object from interesting and contrasting angles. The kinds of questions that might be posed could differ to *What is it?*

Figure 2.5 Example of a feelie box

Figure 2.6 Feelie box in use by the teacher

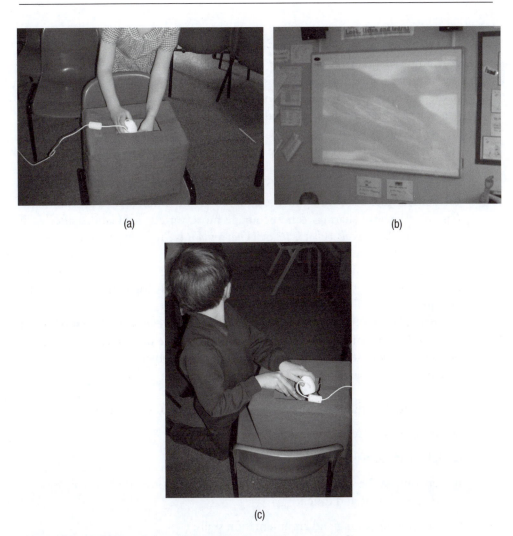

(a)

(b)

(c)

Figure 2.7 (a–c) Feelie box being used by children to ask 'What could it be?'

■ What does it look like?

■ How can you describe it?

■ How is it made?

■ What material might it be? How do you know?

■ Does it look similar to anything else you know?

■ Using your observations and reflecting on the discussions can you suggest what it could be?

■ Why do you suggest this?

Development of scientific understanding and skills

It is important to ensure that the children do not shout out what the object might be in any of the approaches described, but that they are managed (and invited in turn to make suggestions) to enable discussion to emerge (*What can you see?*; *What could that tell us?*) with justifications. Gathering children's descriptions first about what they can see (and later asking for explanations/suggestions) about what the objects/visual image might be often results in eliciting a wider range of ideas from the children. If asking as many children as possible for their views, teachers need to beware of repeated or direct follow-on from each others' ideas. Encouraging the children to contemplate for a few moments (e.g. think before sharing) can encourage more varied speculations after each step of the *Slow reveal, What is it?* or *What could it be?* to help to mediate deeper and more reflective thinking.

Suggestions could be collected and shared on the white board, after each new image is revealed. Conjecture and justified suggestions should be encouraged.

There could be (blind) voting (e.g. hands-up, with eyes closed, to show what they think after various observations) before the whole thing is revealed and the possibilities proposed are contrasted with the actual object.

This 'dramatic' approach has proved to:

■ capture the children's interest in 'unknown' or 'unseen' objects;

■ encourage observational skills;

■ pique curiosity and imagination;

■ encourage the construction of reasoned suggestions based on sensory evidence of sight and touch;

■ develop reasoning and argumentation skills;

■ allow the reflective reviewing of propositions and ideas after 'additional' evidence is presented;

■ encourage students to value ideas of others;

■ manage impulsivity;

■ develop engagement in critical reflection;

■ promote possibility thinking;

■ initiate deeper thinking;

■ provide opportunities to articulate thinking; and

■ allow the application of prior knowledge to 'new' information.

It is also important to think about the way that the object is presented to the children, because they may not engage in careful observation or reasoned creative thinking if the teacher does not 'open' up the discussion to consider any/ or all possibilities.

■ 'What can you see?' is a good opening question. A range of different views from the children can then be gathered. It is important that the children do not think that they have to be 'correct' in what they say; the aim with this technique is to generate creative thought based on keen observations (just as a scientist would).

■ The suggestions from the children can be collated and written on a flipchart or white board, so that the wide range of ideas can be shared.

■ The children can then be asked, 'Why do you think it is like that?'

■ This can then generate a wide range of assorted and interesting responses. What is important is to guide the children to 'justify' their suggestions in a scientific way, e.g. 'I can see it is green and brown, so the plant could be young and old'.

Another approach is to say to the children, 'Each of you in turn will have a chance to say something about the object . . . your sentence will be: "I wonder if . . . because . . ."'.

Everyone is challenged to think about the object then and consider why it might be the way it is. For example, a child might say, 'I wonder if it eats insects, because it has a tube with a lid that could close' or, 'I wonder if is old because it is dry and wizened'.

The suggestions from each child can then be noted and (re)considered when looking even closer at the object. The children can be invited to suggest where else the magnifier needs to focus to possibly help in responding to their ideas.

Conceptual emphasis

Emphasis could be placed on developing or addressing common incomplete or alternate conceptions. For example, many children think that 'seeds' are not alive, that plants only grow from soil in the ground or that magnets possess special glue. The approaches will be more effective if the common misunderstandings within the scientific content are considered and their possible development addressed.

This is probably not too important for this particular strategy, as unusual objects (or common artefacts not usually seen close-up) can throw up incorrect suggestions, but this is encouraged in this approach as long as conjecture is supported by justification.

Using such an open approach can help to link observations to scientific comprehension to ensure that 'scientific understanding' emerges from the dramatic activity. Understandings (and prior learning) about things that are 'alive' or not, or were 'once living' could be explored and revisited at a later point.

Providing such open opportunities can elicit a wide range of children's partial or incomplete understandings (often labelled misconceptions) about things. Exploring children's existing conceptions before teaching a topic is good practice and can inform what to teach or emphasise next. In this way, the on-the-table approach can be used to build a constructivist teaching approach (for a particular topic).

There are various suggestions that could support the topics of 'exploration', 'sports' and 'food' suggested in Tables 2.2, 2.3 and 2.4 below.

Effective questioning and good questions

Questions that only require a 'yes' or 'no' response are not the most motivating to help children to work out what something might be (and indeed, appreciate its importance or how it might be used). For the unusual artefact, e.g. the slow reveal of a helmet, it is not stimulating if the children are asked, 'Do you think it is hard?' or 'Is it black?'; more thoughtful questions could be, 'From the image, what do you think it could it be made of?', 'Why?', 'How can you tell?', 'What could we do to test your idea?'

Question suggestions are listed in Table 2.1.

Assessment opportunities

If children have been taught about some of these ideas earlier then the photographs, images or objects revealed or touched in the feelie box can be chosen purposely to check for learning, e.g. having completed the life cycle of plants, can they recognise seeds, plantlets or fruits? Having finished teaching about materials and their properties, can they identify what is hard/soft; stretchy/stiff; shiny/dull; rough/smooth; bendy/not bendy; waterproof/not waterproof; absorbent/not absorbent, etc.? Having completed a topic on light can they apply words such as transparent, translucent and opaque to different reflective/none reflective materials?

Reflections from the classroom

Children are very imaginative and apply a whole range of ideas to interpret and explain what they see. The example of pitcher plant images was used with children to introduce looking at and thinking about an unfamiliar object.

Comments from the children include: 'I thought it was from the ice age', 'I thought it was an old plant', 'I thought the long tube could trap something', 'I thought it was from the stone age', 'It had like a big hole with a lid on . . . which gave me the idea of a trap', 'I thought it was a crab because it looked like it had pincers.'

Presenting interesting and magnified images can really stir the imagination and engage the children in reflecting about what something might be and offering a suggestion about why.

A teacher indicated that she thought: 'On the table is very good for inquiry, asking questions, observation, "what if" sort of questions and looking at the intricate working of something . . . getting the children to use good language for description and investigation' (year five teacher, North Staffordshire school).

Further suggestions

These are included in the following table that describes when on the table might be useful for teaching the themes of exploration, sports and food.

TABLE 2.2 Applying 'on the table' to an exploration theme – some examples

Strategy	Description of strategy	Key learning objectives	Activities	Question starters
On the table: What could it be?	Examining objects (often unusual or to be used in an unusual way) Teacher or children scan the object under the Easiscope/digital microscope/visualiser. The teacher models open questions – What could it be? Why is it that colour? I wonder what it might be used for?	To explore objects, to speculate and evaluate evidence to identify objects. To observe and listen carefully. To take turns and share ideas.	Place an interesting object e.g. gourd into a bag. Slowly reveal using the Easiscope to support the development of observation skills. Questions that could be asked include: *What could it be?* *Why do you think it is that?* *What does a . . . look like?* *Any other ideas?* Revealed a bit at a time. *Could it be a . . .?* *A . . . has . . . . Has this got . . .?* *What might it be?* *Which questions are answered by the physical appearance of the object?* *What further information might we need to identify/be sure . . .?*	What could it . . .? What might it . . .? What further information might we need . . .? What do other people think?
On the table: Hide and show	Group/s are presented with an unknown object hidden in a box. The teacher models open questions – What could it be? Why is it that colour? I wonder what it might be used for?	To raise questions. To explore and collect evidence to describe the unusual specimen.	Teacher/another pupil is a plant hunter returned from an expedition with an unusual specimen. With the children in a circle, the plant hunter gathers the children round and introduces them to the specimens, e.g. pitcher plant. *What do you think these are? What might they be? Are they alive or dead? Animal or plant?* The teacher, in role, models and describes aspects of the specimens. The children are scientists and have their notebooks. The teacher encourages them to record in their own way, e.g. 'It is in soil. Let's write it down/did you make a record of that?' *Are there any bits that are not so alive?* *Why might that be?*	What do you think . . .? What might they be? How do you know? How might we find out?

How does it feel? Should we touch it? It might have toxic sap!

What questions have you got?

Is there something in the pod?

Why is it that shape?

Does it eat things?

What could we do to find out about its shape?

Does it live in a hot place/cold place?

Are insects attracted to it? How might that be?

What doesn't it have? Any flowers?

Has it got liquid inside?

How could we find out?

On the table: Close scrutiny	Examining objects (often unusual or to be used in an unusual way).	To explore objects and speculate how they might be used.	The children are on an imaginary beach. Items are placed to make a strandline, e.g. seaweed, driftwood, bright material, netting, shells, old bucket, plastic knife, shiny metal, spade.	What could it . . .?
		To consider and evaluate the usefulness of objects in producing sound and/or light for different purposes.	In pairs, children choose an item they think will help them to survive. They do not pick it up.	What might it . . .?
	Group/s are presented with an object under the Easiscope/digital microscope/visualiser. The teacher models open questions – What could it be? Why is it that colour? I wonder what it might be used for?		Pair by pair, ask the children to pick up the item and give a reason for their choice. What will they do if someone else picks up the object they wanted?	I wonder if . . .?
		To apply understanding of materials, sound and light to solve different problems.	Tell the children that there is a boat passing.	What happens if you . . .?
		To observe and listen carefully.	Ask the children to role play how they might use the item chosen to ensure that they might be noticed.	What makes it good for . . .?
		To take turns and share ideas.	E.g. Children might wave the brightly coloured materials, they might hit the spade with a stone, reflect light off a tin.	What do other people think?
			Share ideas. Did they pick the object up with that in mind . . . or not?	
			Challenge the children to role play how they might use the item if they had to make a shelter, to make a raft. What makes that object good for that purpose?	

TABLE 2.3 Applying 'on the table' to a sports theme – some examples

Strategy	Description of strategy	Key learning objectives	Activities	Question starters
On the table: What is it?	Examining objects (often unusual or to be used in an unusual way). Group/s are presented with an object under the Easiscope/ digital microscope/ visualiser. The teacher models open questions – What could it be? Why is it that colour? I wonder what it might be used for?	To explore objects, to speculate and evaluate evidence to identify objects. To observe and listen carefully. To take turns and share ideas.	Ask children to sit in groups. Model using a feelie bag/box with the whole group. Place the material, e.g. brick, wool, pumice, sponge. Ensure the children have not seen it. Ask a child to feel the object. Possible questions to ask: *How does it feel?* *What does it feel like?* *What happens if you press it?* *Is it hard/soft? How do you know?* *How does it feel if you stroke it?* *What material do you think it is?* *What do you think will happen if you pull it . . . press it?* *How do you think this material might be used? What might it be used for? Why would it be good for that?* Pass the feelie bag along – can the next child add to the description? Can anyone guess what the object is? Develop the activity to use several feelie boxes for the children to use in groups. Children could compare and contrast the objects. Several different balls made of different materials could be used. What sport is it used for and why?	How does it feel? Can you think of anything else it feels like? What happens if you . . .? What could it . . .? What might it . . .? What further information might we need . . .? What do other people think?
On the table: Slow reveal	Group/s are presented with an object. The teacher models open questions – What	To raise questions. To explore and collect evidence to	Ask the children to sit as a class. What clothing might be in the bag? Place an object in a bag. Set up the Easiscope/visualiser/digital microscope and use it to reveal a part of the object a bit at a time. The children should develop a description and use this to try to identify the object. Children to give descriptive words. Ask questions such as:	What do you think . . .? What might they be?

could it be? Why is it that colour? I wonder what it might be used for? Children ask questions.	describe the unusual object.	*What does this suggest? How do you know?* *What object might be . . .?* *What does that tell you?* *What kind of material do you think it is?* *What makes you think it has . . .?* *If it is a . . . would it . . .?* Examples of objects: hockey face guard, cricket pads, running spikes.	How do you know? How might we find out?
On the table: Close scrutiny	Group/s are presented with an object. The teacher models open questions – What could it be? Why is it that colour? I wonder what it might be used for? Children ask questions.	To use senses to gather evidence to describe and compare the materials that objects are made of. To identify how science is used in the development of objects we use.	*Teacher in role. Found this object in the attic, e.g. old tennis racket/modern tennis racket.* Pass it around. Ask questions such as: *What can you tell me about it?* *What might it be?* *What do you think it is used for?* *What is it made of?* *Is it wood/is it metal? How do you know?* *Why do you think it is made out of this material?* *Do you recognise the object?* *How is it different to the modern object?* *How old do you think it is? Why do you think that?* *Was plastic invented then?* *Is it light or heavy?* *What else could it be made of?* *Where do you think it is used?* *Do you think it is all here?* (Other old and modern objects that could be used – swimming costumes, footballs, hot water bottles, dolls.)	What can you tell me about . . .? What might it be? What do you think it is used for? How do you know? How might we find out? How old do you think it is? Why?

TABLE 2.4 Applying 'on the table' to a food theme – an example

Strategy	Description of strategy	Key learning objectives	Activities	Question starters
On the table: What is it?	Examining seeds, fruits (often unusual or to be used in an unusual way). Group/s are presented with an object under the Easiscope/digital microscope/visualiser. The teacher models open questions – What could it be? Why is it that colour? I wonder what it might be used for?	To explore objects, to speculate and evaluate. To observe and listen carefully. To take turns and share ideas.	Ask questions, such as: What do you think this is? Do you think these are alive or dead? Can you tell if they are alive or dead? How could we find out? If I planted these seeds what do you think these will grow into? Why do you think that? Can you see any evidence that tells us what they grew from? What does it look like has happened? What has emerged? What do you think that is? What do you think this seed might grow into? How different are these to the other seeds? What food might this be? Would you like to eat this food?	What could it . . .? What might it . . .? What do you think? Do you think . . .? What do other people think? How could we . . .?

3

Spontaneous role play

Introduction to the approach

Being spontaneous in a learning situation provides the opportunity for the children to think, act and talk in situations where there is no one correct answer. Engaging with spontaneous role-play, learners can take on a particular perspective, role or character and improvise within a given situation or scenario. By discussing and working in-role, learners are able to explore views and ideas that may be different to their own.

Experiences that children have of science in schools are often aimed at children developing a particular aspect of knowledge or developing specific science skills. When children are asked to apply these skills and understanding to the context given (e.g. *What do penguins eat? Fish*; or *What force moves a suitcase? Push*; or *What makes ice melt? Heat*) the teacher often holds in their mind a narrow set of expected responses. In the everyday world, in order to solve a problem we often, however, need to draw on a much wider range of knowledge and life experiences. Solving a problem might involve identifying what the problem is, imagining what a successful outcome might look like, thinking about other similar problems that have been solved before, considering different peoples' opinions, knowing that there are different possible outcomes and being able to evaluate which is the best solution. The questions above, for example, could be broadened to consider: *What could penguins eat, when injured and taken into the zoo to be cared for?*; *What forces could move a suitcase across different types of ground found on a desert island?*; *What can prevent ice (for example, an ice rink) melting in the summer?* Spontaneous role play, therefore, can be employed to engage children in thinking about science in an everyday context. In real-world situations, then, it can support children exploring different possibilities to solve a problem, engage in deliberation over what these might mean and subsequently agree solutions.

General development of scientific understanding and skills through role play

Spontaneous role play enables children to empathise with different views and perspectives about ideas and concepts in science. Aubusson and Fogwill (2006) also indicate how it promotes elevated discussion. This is because it allows children to stand in the shoes of a different person or take on a part, role or character and explore how that person/object might act or behave in different situations. For example, the situation might be a child finding a 'sweet' or a bottle of brightly coloured liquid. The roles might be a child who may want to eat or drink the 'sweet' or 'drink', other friends, a parent or a nurse. The children can then explore that dilemma from the different viewpoints. *What should they do? What options are available? Should they eat the 'sweet'? What else might it be? What harm could it do? What might happen if they ate the sweet?* This kind of spontaneous role play prompts the children's thinking to try and solve a problem; in doing so their thoughts can become apparent through their discussion. Listening to their deliberations and observing their improvisation can illuminate the way in which they perceive a solution might be reached. Inferences about scientific understandings can be made from the dialogic exchanges. McSharry and Jones (2002) have described the ways in which role play can offer cognitive development as well as promote understanding about how science works.

Guidance to use 'spontaneous role play'

Theme 1: Exploration

This is a technique that works well if children work in groups of three or four. The children can be told that they are on a desert island (the boat ran aground on a trip) and it is getting dark. The technique mind-movies (Chapter 8) can bring this setting alive. The classroom could be set-up to recreate an authentic environment: the room in blackout, ice and/or dried seaweed to feel, sounds of howling wolves, screaming winds, owls, bats, waves. The children, working in groups, can be encouraged to use their senses, and their imagination, to make suggestions as to where (and what) this place might be (like). They can be asked, *What can you see/hear/smell? What can you tell you about this place? What might live here?* The teacher can add further information i.e. *I can see . . . Can anyone else see . . . ? What do you think it can be?* As the children add their ideas it will build up a description of this place.

The children can then be asked to discuss and identify what questions they would need to ask if they were to stay in this place overnight; e.g. If we had to stay in the place overnight, *What would we need to think about?*; *What would we eat?*; *What food might there be?*; *What could we drink?*; *Where might we get something to drink?*; *Is it safe to drink/eat it?*; *How can we keep dry/warm/cool?*; *What might we find that is useful?*, etc. Once these questions have been agreed they can be sorted into themes, e.g. food, water, shelter, safety, light, comfort. Each group can be given a question or group of questions to discuss. They can be asked to role play being explorers who have been marooned on the island and they need to discuss what they would do to address the question/questions for their given responsibility. For example, for the shelter they might need to discuss where is the best place to build it: would it be on the beach, in the woods, on a hill, on flat ground, in grass, on sand? They will also need to think about what they might find that could be used to build the shelter: rocks, branches, sand or soil? They will also need to consider the roof, and what they might need for that: pebbles, leaves, plastic sheeting found on the beach, seaweed or ferns? The children should be encouraged to discuss and explore a number of possible alternatives. It is also useful to add some unsuitable materials to promote discussion and elicit understanding. The children can then contemplate why some materials might be better than others, and why others are less suitable. This can be supported by having a series of objects that are washed up on the strand line (see Figure 3.1) on the beach, which can serve as a stimulus for thinking of ways to help them survive. The beauty of this is that the tide can bring in 'new materials' to use as the teacher wishes.

Extending learning

In their groups of four, each family/friendship group member can be given a card which has a particular need, e.g. one person is really sensitive to the sun, another is petrified of creepy crawlies, one person really wants to get off the island and another does not like getting cold. Asking the children how they might alter a shelter to accommodate all these people would require a rethink. *What do they need to mull over now? Would they use the same materials? Why might they choose different materials? What properties are more important now? Would they build it in the same place? Why/Why not? How else could they build it? What might be different, what might be the same? Is there anything they know about already that might help?*

REFLECTIVE DISCUSSION

On completion of the task the children can be encouraged to think about how well the shelter met the needs of the different members of the group. *Does it keep the person sensitive to the sun safe? Would it stop creepy crawlies getting in/keep the person warm? What different materials did they use and why? How did building the shelter help the person who really wants to go home? How did they encourage them? Did they take part? How did they feel? How did they make others feel? Would they all*

Figure 3.1 A model strandline

like to be marooned on a desert island? What would be good about it? What would be bad about it?

Development of skills and understandings

Children involved in this activity can become engaged and motivated in discussion. The nature of the spontaneous role play can encourage the children to explore alternatives and justify decisions. Children who had been camping drew on their experiences of sleeping under canvas and living in a rural situation. Children suggested and developed plans that ensured everyone's needs were met.

Figure 3.2 A year five class adopting characters from a Katie Morag book and going for a coastal walk. A baby seal is hurt and washed up on the beach. A tourist tries to feed it biscuits. Others throw litter on the beach. The children consider, discuss and enact what they would do

Figure 3.3 Children in role 'selling' the properties and suitability of their chosen materials

They also thought carefully about everyday life. Teachers found this convention worked better if it was introduced gradually with one problem at a time until children became more familiar with the technique.

The teachers felt that role play was an effective tool. It was reported that it was particularly useful in finding out what the children's ideas were, in developing reasoning and problem solving skills and in encouraging the children to work well as a team. One teacher found that it showed children clearly how we, as humans, are very adaptable. The impact was difficult to quantify; the teachers observed that it developed questioning, reasoning and reflection skills. It was observed to be particularly useful for those children with special needs, and these children benefitted far more as they could voice opinions and ask questions.

Spontaneous role play proved more challenging for some teachers. When children role-played building a shelter, they discussed possible places to make it as well as considering how to construct it. Children became engrossed in the spontaneous role play and could be seen sawing down trees, dragging branches, knocking in pegs, becoming physically tired and hanging their heads after the exertion of the imagined activity. Other children carried bricks one after the other, slowly stacking them higher and higher, some threw imaginary sheets of material over branches and secured them with pegs. The children appeared to be more secure in doing one task themselves rather than working together to collaboratively build a den (indicating that they found it easier to draw on real-life personal experience rather than 'imagine how' they might do something unfamiliar).

Reflections from the classroom

One teacher shared that, 'I think the role play is good as an extra. It develops thought processes and if you sit back and listen to what they [the children] have to say you can see where they are in their learning. It's not directed. You are giving them a little bit and then they run with it, which is one of the big advantages of using drama in science. It's more children-led . . . and you can be surprised by what they have to say' (year five teacher, North Staffordshire school).

Theme 2: Animals

Children can be organised into small groups, e.g. five per group. Either give or let the children choose an animal that they would like to look after in the zoo. Ask them to research information about their animal. Ask them to imagine that they are in the role of the zoo keepers for their chosen animal and that they are now responsible for looking after their animal. *What will they need to do to look after their animal? What does it eat? How much space does it need? What might that space look like? What will they do to look after that animal? How many animals have they got in their enclosure? How many times a day do they eat? How much do they eat? Do they eat the same food every day? How are they fed? What else do they need apart from food?* Then, as a spontaneous role play (see Figure 3.2), how would they organise a day round the zoo so that everyone gets a chance to see the different animals? What would the children need to think about? The scenario could be that the zoo is at the planning stage so that they have to think about the size and organisation of the enclosures, or the children could be given a map of the zoo and organise the route considering what times the animals are more likely to be asleep and feeding times. Ideally this would be linked to an educational visit to a zoo/animal park so that the children could find out the information about the role of the keepers, the behaviour and needs of the animals and/or needs of the visitors.

Extending learning further

Learning can be extended further by setting '*What if?*' situations for the children to consider in a role play. The children can remain in the role of zookeeper for their particular animal, but they are one member of the zoo management team and together they have to work out how to solve the different issues (below in Table 3.1) that may arise.

Development of scientific understanding and skills

Being given the role of zoo keeper gives a real purpose to find out exactly what the needs of that animal might be. It gives a reason to research the needs of the animal since the role play is 'performed'. The impact of this is that the children are highly motivated. The strategy draws on prior understanding, which becomes more explicit when teachers observe how far children appreciate what living things need to survive. Children, role playing the more expert zoo keeper, can became more critical of information they have read in books. The 'what if' scenarios encourage broader thinking about different

TABLE 3.1 Examples of situation cards you could give the groups to consider

Possible situations – what would you do?
The man who delivers the fish has not arrived. There are no fish for any of the animals to eat.
One of the tigers has escaped from its pen.
Children have been found feeding sweets to animals all around the zoo.
A family are having a picnic and are throwing all the litter into the water in the crocodile enclosure.
A parent is complaining that it is unfair to keep the polar bear in its cage.
There has been so much rain that all the animal pens in the zoo are filling up with water – they are flooding.

aspects of science. The children might start by thinking all animals eat the same as humans, but should develop their understanding, through discussion, that animals eat different foods and that some animals have more varied diets than others. It may be that the children need to have time to research what the animals need in order to have the knowledge to role play. Problem solving what happens when there is only fish encourages team work. Some children might not feel that it is important to them, as their animal does not eat fish, so they have to revisit their thinking, taking into account the views of other zoo keepers. Role playing what to do when the tiger escapes encourages the children to think of the risks and to explore ways of reducing the risk. They have to apply their understanding of tigers, their needs, their behaviour and the needs of the visitors and other animals of the zoo. In discussing it, they need to be able to put their view forward and begin to justify their ideas. This allows them to collaboratively develop their knowledge and understanding. Role playing feeding the animals and not leaving litter develops the sense of responsibility and helps the children to appreciate reasons behind (animal care and zoo keeping) rules. A flooding problem at the zoo encourages identifying which animals would be most at risk and why. Again children have to 'know their animal', be able to justify why their animal might be more or less at risk and then be open to the ideas of others in order to provide a solution to suit all the animals. Using spontaneous role play in this kind of situation supports children to develop understanding of the similarities and differences between the habitats and diets of different animals and of the roles of zoos, safari parks and nature reserves. Table 3.2 summarises suggestions about how this convention could be used to promote understanding about animals.

Reflections from the classroom

Feedback from teachers trialling role play as a learning tool varied. Some teachers felt that it made science learning fun and uncovered what the children did not understand, while others felt that the children asked the questions too quickly and then engagement fell. Reflection revealed that the children required some practise to participate in spontaneous role play, as children at the outset found it difficult to communicate viewpoints other than their own. However the technique developed children's ideas that there are alternate perspectives and that situations are often more complex than they initially thought. As the children practised, the relevance and focus of the questions they asked each other improved. Some teachers found it difficult to apply the convention in situations other than that given, others felt more confident. One teacher gave the children cards of information on each animal and a range of habitats. She then asked the children to role play setting up a zoo. The children were then asked to decide who will live with whom and the

TABLE 3.2 Applying spontaneous role play to an animals theme

Strategy	Description of strategy	Key learning objectives	Activities	Question starters
Spontaneous role play: Zookeepers	In small groups, children develop arguments about science in everyday life. By working 'in role' they can explore views and ideas that may be different from their own.	To consider what living things need to survive. To explore ideas and possibilities about how to look after living things. To take turns. To listen to others' speaking.	Divide the children into small groups, e.g. five per group. Give each child an animal they are zoo keeper for. They need to appreciate that they are responsible for all the care that animal will need. Discuss and plan for the care of x animal for a day. What will you need to do? Consider the following: *What do they eat? When? How much? How do they feed?* *What else do they need apart from food?* *What kind of shelter do they need in their pen?* *How much space do they need?* *Can they share their pen with others?*	What might they need . . .? How often might they . . .? How much should they . . .? How much should we . . .? How might we . . .? What else might they . . .? How might we find out . . .?

best place for each animal to live. This proved really useful in identifying what children knew or did not know. A further example was to dilemma whether frogspawn brought into school (to study life cycles) should be kept (for several weeks in the class aquarium to observe the metamorphosis of tadpoles) or be returned back to the pond. This brought out some interesting comments from children, including, 'I think we should let them hatch so we can see how they grow'. Another said 'No I think they should be put back in the pond so they can, like, live their life' (year six class, North Staffordshire school).

Theme 3: Sports

In this theme the children take on the roles of 'buyers' and 'sellers' (of materials for sports clothing) in an imaginary market place (see Figure 3.3). The children can be asked to work in groups of three. The class can be divided into two teams and asked to choose three materials that they think would be suitable to make the sports clothing for their Olympic team (of rowers; cyclists; swimmers, etc.). One half of the class are the sellers (or shop keepers) and their role is to *persuade* the buyers to purchase their materials. The sellers need to be able to explain to the buyers why their materials are suitable for different sports (flexible, waterproof, hard wearing, good insulator, etc.). The groups of buyers can be told that they need to choose only *one* material (that best suits their needs) that they think will be suitable to make clothes for their Olympic team. It is useful to have each group explain to the class, in turn, which material they would buy and why.

The market place role play is best done after the monologue (Appendix 13) and follow-up investigation (exploring a range of materials such as sponge, bubble wrap, cotton, elastic, card, etc.) and the children should be asked, 'What can you find out about the material?' and 'How can you find out which is the best for an Olympic sportsperson to wear?'

Extending learning further

The task can be extended by increasing the number of materials considered and discussing why they might be useful for different parts of sports clothing, e.g. harder wearing materials for elbows and knees, more breathable materials for areas where the body gets hot and sticky (sweaty).

Development of scientific understanding and skills

The children really enjoyed the shop element and the spontaneous role play supported them in justifying why a certain material was useful for a particular purpose. Actually selling and buying the material really made the learning relevant and gave it authenticity. It was important for children to see both sides of the role, e.g. as seller and buyer. The sports clothing market place supported children in making close observations of the various fabrics, exploring how it felt against the skin, whether it stretched well, how flexible it was and whether it would stand up to a lot of wear and tear. It also supported more innovative thinking as they began to imagine how they might test the materials, and some considered whether it would soak up sweat well and how they might test this phenomenon. It really promoted the children's questioning skills and the use of scientific vocabulary. Children were observed modelling how flexible the material was by wrapping it around their wrist. They also 'sold' the material by describing a particular property and suggesting why that property would be useful for clothing for a specific sport: 'This material would be good because it stretches as you move' and 'if you were running and sweating a lot this material would be cool' (year four class, South Staffordshire school). The spontaneous role play also led to improvisation with the children in roles challenging the 'seller' with such questions as *What if you fell over, how protective would this material be?* These questions and the responses offered enabled the teachers to evaluate the children's understanding of the properties of the materials and their suitability for the clothing.

Theme 4: Food

Situation 1

The children can be organised in groups of four. Ask or suggest the roles that the children could take in a family, e.g. mum, dad, brother and sister. Each person is given a 'concern' card. These could be: *You are a vegetarian*; *You are allergic to peanuts*; *You do not like brown bread*; *You can't eat bananas*, etc. The children can then be challenged to role play agreeing what they might put in a healthy packed lunch (or picnic) that everyone could eat.

Situation 2

The children can be organised in groups of four. Each group is a family and the children can choose who will be who in the family, e.g. one child could be mother, another father, another an older sibling, etc. The children could be asked to imagine that they are a family in a supermarket buying food for a meal. There may be a diabetic or gluten allergy sufferer, a toddler, a pregnant mum, a vegetarian. Food choices will depend on the roles adopted. The groups can then act out the discussion and eventually agree on what they will buy in the supermarket to make a healthy family meal.

Development of scientific understanding and skills

Spontaneous role play proved a useful tool to extend appreciation of a healthy lunch. The discussion can uncover misunderstandings such as a lunch being healthy if it was solely vegetables or salad. It developed appreciation that you need a variety of foods for a healthy diet. In addition, children had to back up their ideas with reasons and agree a consensus in the group as what to eventually buy.

Reflections from the classroom: spontaneous role play generally

This technique proved very useful in identifying children's current understanding. While learning about Borneo, for example, in a tropical rain forest topic, and asked to make their shelters, children's understanding of the materials available in the different habitats could be easily identified by observation and listening. Careful observation of children's interactions can illuminate their conceptual understanding, so that teachers may recognise when it is appropriate to intervene and step in to ask a question or to challenge ideas. This approach uncovers beliefs and perceptions about properties of the fabrics by watching how the children mimed using the materials. Observations indicated that some children and teachers had little experience of foam and thus were unsure of its properties. One teacher felt that a costume made of foam would not make any difference to swimming; a child thought that thick foam might stop you moving as well, and that once bent it might stay like that. This gave an opportunity to investigate the properties of that particular material, so that they could develop their understanding of the properties of a foam sponge further.

4

Hot seating

Introduction

Hot seating is a technique where teachers or learners are placed 'in role' and questioned about being that character, object or living organism. A teacher or child in the hot seat can also 'be' someone reflecting on a particular event or experience. The person in the 'hot seat' usually sits on a chair and is somewhat in the 'spotlight' when questioned by the others in class. Other learners ask the 'hot seated' character(s) questions (see Figure 4.1). The person in-role in the hot seat might be an expert, a character with a point of view or an object or living thing that others are asking questions about/of.

Developing children's appreciation that in science often there may be a range of responses or solutions to a problem is the essence of the nature of science (e.g. to 'boil' a liquid you can heat it, but you could also cause a similar visual effect through increasing the pressure or adding a reactive solid; most children would probably think that only applying heat could cause a liquid to 'bubble' at the surface).

Hot seating can be a useful technique to develop this way of thinking as it allows children to explore a scientific idea from a number of perspectives. As a learning technique it is highly personalised as it starts from the questions that learners would like to ask about an idea, scientific concept, event or happening. It is also a technique that can bring science alive and can demonstrate the relevance of science to the everyday lives of people either in the present or in the past.

Hot seating allows teachers and children to explore what might be behind the thinking of a character. It can be used to examine the ideas that a character holds and the reasoning that shapes decisions that character has made. It can be used to develop both understanding and skills. It can help learning to become more relevant as the children can ask questions that they want to find the answers to that are more personally pertinent for them. The person being asked the questions is also challenged by the questions other learners ask, which can often broaden their thinking and deepen their understanding, too.

Figure 4.1 A group being 'hot seated' that followed on from the role play (Figure 3.2: a coastal walk). The children in the class have devised questions to ask those in the 'hot seats'. The children being hot seated have to justify their responses and points of view

A group of children could be hot seated after they have 'done' something, for example, after miming how to play a sport in different material clothing, e.g. wearing a foil shirt to play football, or playing netball with an ice ball, the children can answer questions about 'how it was for them!'

Guidance to using 'hot seating'

Theme 1: Animals

The children can be asked to discuss in groups what they think the role/job of a zoo keeper is. Thy can then be asked to imagine they are zoo keepers and consider: *What kind of animal might they want to look after?*; *What would they need to know to be able to care for that animal properly?*; *What will it need to keep healthy?*; *What will they have to do to look after it?* The children could do some research and make their own fact file on the animal they could be asked (or choose) to be responsible for. Alternatively, children could be given a number of animal fact files and select one. Learning could be supported and enriched by a visit to a zoo (or even a farm and adopt the role of a livestock farmer) to provide the children with the real experiences and knowledge that they would need to imagine themselves in the role of zoo keeper. Once the children are familiar with the needs of their chosen animal they can then be told that there is a group of children coming to look around the zoo and that they would like to ask the zoo keeper some questions about the care of the animals. It was found to be helpful for children to be placed in small groups in order to formulate the questions about how to look after the animal(s).

Hot seating: children as experts

Ask the 'zookeeper' to sit in the 'hot seat'. 'Hot seat' the zookeepers to find out what they think their animals need (food, water, shelter, habitat, etc.).

Extending thinking

Learning can be further extended by giving the children a challenge. For example, *What if . . . the zoo has run out of fish?;. . . the weather has become very cold?;. . . some children from one of the schools has dropped litter into the cage of an animal?; . . . a child has fed one of the animals some food?* Ask the children to choose a child to hot seat to explore possible issues that these actions might raise and possible solutions to the problems.

Hot seating: teacher as expert

Learning could be extended still further by giving the children a final problem: a baby seal has been found on the beach. It seems very poorly. What questions would we need to ask? The teacher can take the role of the zoo manager. The children in role as zoo keepers can consider what questions they might want to ask the zoo manager. *What are the dangers of bringing the poorly seal into the zoo or not? Do we know what is making it ill? Could other animals 'catch' the illness? What will it eat? Who would be best at looking after the animal? Where else could the seal be taken? Is the zoo the best place for the animal?* This could be followed by hot seating the zoo keepers of different animals. *Do they want to help the seal? Why/ why not? How would this affect the animal they are looking after?* The children could then develop a solution.

Developing of skills and understanding

In this scenario hot seating provided a vehicle to explore the children's understanding of the needs of their chosen animal. By answering questions from other children they had to think more carefully and in more detail. The children saw the relevance of knowing the needs in order to look after their chosen animal. It resulted in a deeper thinking as the children were challenged further to think of other ways to meet the needs when problems arose. Hot seating also provided an opportunity to develop higher order thinking skills through experiencing and considering different viewpoints and evaluating possible solutions.

Theme 2: Sports

In this scenario, the children are Olympic athletes. They need to buy materials to make the clothes for the athletes. In groups allow the children to explore and test the different materials in groups. Allow the children opportunities to sort the materials according to their properties, e.g. waterproof, stretchy, breathable, silky, smooth, flexible, absorbent. Ask the children to choose three materials that would be suitable to make the clothes for the athletes. Split the class into two halves. Now tell the children to imagine the classroom as a market. Tell one half that they each have a stall from which to 'sell' their three chosen materials to the Olympic Committee. The other half are 'buyers' and need to decide which of the materials they will buy.

Hot seating: children as experts

In this scenario the children can be 'hot seated' as the expert 'sellers' – since they have knowledge of the properties of the materials – or expert 'buyers' – since they know the properties of the materials they need to 'buy'. *Which materials did they choose and why? Would their materials be good for any other sports? Why do they think that?*

Extending thinking

What if the committee say that the chosen material is too expensive? What alternative material might the group choose instead? How might the material be improved so that it might appeal to more sportsmen and women?

Hot seating: teacher as expert

The children could 'hot seat' the teacher as an expert from a sportswear manufacturing company. The children could be given the challenge of making clothing for an unfamiliar sport new to the games. They could also be asked to explore items of clothing where different materials have been used for different parts of the clothing. The challenge for the children is to then construct questions to ask the hot-seated (teacher) expert so that they better understand why different materials have been used for particular clothing.

Development of skills and understanding

Children found the 'market place' element highly engaging. Hot seating in the role of 'seller' clarified children's thinking on the properties of materials and gave opportunities to rehearse describing the materials and giving reasons for their arguments on why a material would be suitable for this or that task. As 'buyers' the children were able to develop their questioning skills as they challenged 'sellers' on the suitability of the materials for different sports. Being in the 'hot seat' as a 'buyer' and 'seller' helped the children to see the necessity of knowing about the properties of materials. Hot seating the 'buyers' helped to identify children's understanding of the properties of the materials they bought.

Theme 3: A Victorian garden

In this scenario, the children imagine that they are going back in time, to the time of the Victorians. They are visiting the garden of a big house. They are going to interview the gardener. The teacher or other adult is dressed up as a Victorian gardener, e.g. a flat cap, waistcoat, shirt and trousers with a gardening fork or spade. Ask the children what questions they might want to ask the gardener. These questions can be modelled by the teacher: *I wonder what a Victorian gardener would grow in his garden?*; *I wonder what he might eat?*; *Where do you think people got their food in the past?*; *How was food from the garden kept fresh (as there were no fridges or freezers then)?*

The children work in pairs to come up with questions to ask the Victorian gardener.

Hot seating: teacher as expert

The teacher is introduced as the Victorian gardener and the children ask their questions. Examples of the questions they might ask could include:
What do you do?; *Where do people get their food from?*; *Where do you get your food from?*; *What kinds of things do you grow?*; *Do you eat any of the things that are grown in the garden?*; *Who decides what you grow?*; *How do you decide where to grow different things?*; *What do you do if you grow too much?*; *Are there any plants that you do not grow? Why not?*; *Are there any fruit or vegetables you would like to grow?*; *What is growing in your garden now?*; *What fruit and vegetables have you got a lot of now?*

Extending learning

The children could be told that the Victorian family are moving to a different country. It is very hot, and they could be encouraged to think about the questions that you might ask the gardener. *What would you grow then? What problems might you have? Which vegetables and fruit would you still grow? Which would be more difficult to grow?*

This could be an introductory activity to growing different vegetables and fruit or comparing germinating seeds in a range of temperatures (window sill, in fridge, etc.).

Hot seating: children as experts

Hot seat the children as gardeners. They could be asked: *Which vegetables and fruit would you still grow?*; *Which would be more difficult? Why?*

Development of skills and understanding

Hot seating the gardener proved to be very engaging for year six students. The children realised that they needed to use the right vocabulary for the expert to understand the questions. Children's questioning skills no ticeably improved and children developed a deeper understanding of where fruit and vegetables come from. It also highlighted children's ideas on germination and growth, allowing them to clarify the differences between what seeds need to germinate and what seedlings need to grow. The children developed a better understanding of how, where and why various fruits grow in different climates.

Theme 4: Exploration

The final scenario is a desert island. The children can imagine that they have been shipwrecked on a desert island. The children can be told it is getting darker and they need to build a shelter. Here the children can hot seat another survivor who has been on the island for some time and already has a good shelter. The children can talk in pairs and agree some questions that they could put to the expert.

Hot seating: teacher as expert

The survivor is in the hot seat. They can be questioned to explore how they have survived. *How did they make it? What tips would they be willing to share?* The expert in this case might mime or show children how to join, break, whittle branches and how to make twine from leaves. The expert might ask the children to mime with them. *How did they make it?* The 'expert' might also model the use of scientific words that describe the effects of different forces such as push, pull, twist, stretch, squash and squeeze.

Extending thinking

Learning can be extended through 'what ifs': *What if there is a storm?*; *How can we keep ourselves safe from . . . small insects?*; . . . too much sunlight?*

Development of skills, understanding and dispositions

The children developed a deeper understanding of the use of plants; for example, that leaves and vines can be used for different purposes. The children also developed their imaginative and questioning skills by asking how the shelter might be improved against wind and rain.

Questions stems useful to develop hot seating

Should we . . .?
What might happen if . . .?
Why do we think . . .?
What should we choose? Why?
What might you . . .?
How could you . . .?
What would you choose? Why?
What might you . . .?
How could you . . .?

Conceptual development

Hot seating could be used at the beginning or end of a topic or sequence of teaching to assess what the children know and/or understand at the onset of teaching something . . . or as a culminatory activity checking what they have learned through engaging with a particular topic or theme.

Reflections from the classroom

If the children are to be the expert then it is important to ensure that they have sufficient life experience or knowledge of that role. This can be addressed by:

- educational visits or visitors relevant to the scenario;

- giving opportunities for older children to mentor younger children; or

- setting up opportunities for the children to do detailed research or experimenting before the drama work.

Further hot-seating suggestions

The hot-seated person could be in the role of:

- a seed underground, and be asked: *What is happening around you as you grow?*; *What can you see/feel/hear?*

- an animal in its habitat, and be asked: *Why do you live here?*; *What can you see/feel/hear?*

- a particular animal, and be asked (about its shape and structure): *Why do you have . . . big ears?*; *. . . sharp claws?*

- a musical instrument, and be asked: *How is sound made from you?*; *What are you made of?*; *Is what you are made of important to make sounds?*

- a shadow, and be asked: *How are you created?*; *What is around you?*; *Where is the . . . sun?*; *. . . light coming from?*

- as children (or another living creature or a once alive thing) of different ages, and be asked: *How do you know how old you are?*; *How different are you . . . when you are young?*; *. . . when you are old?*

- as a toy, and be asked: *What makes you move?*; *How could you be made to move differently?*

5

Miming movement

Introduction to the approach

This approach adopts the use of whole body movements or actions to mime (without words, although representative sounds can be used) scientific ideas or suggestions. It can be used, for example to illustrate the flow of an electrical current, the development of a germinating seed or what happens to molecules during the change of state of different substances. If children are asked to engage in this to show *their views or interpretations*, then it is not modelling in the strict sense, because they may be improvising (rather than replicating a concept). Through adopting this approach it is possible to activate children's prior understanding through their consideration and decision-making about how to move. Taking turns to *show* your group's (or individual) mime(s) can then be adapted to examine that movement in detail under different conditions or circumstances that are often not practical or possible in the classroom, e.g. moving a very heavy object, walking on the moon or showing how skating might change as the ice rink melts. Reflective discussion can celebrate original, clear enactments and help focus on the interpretations and meanings of the varied representative actions.

For children to become good scientific thinkers we need them to be curious and to wonder. We aspire for them to be so engaged (and reflective) that they constantly ask questions about what happens and why so that they deepen their understanding about the world around them and beyond. At the same time, as teachers, we need to be able to grasp the depth of their understanding in order to ask that important next question or scaffold that exciting next step. Knowing what you understand and what you do not understand can be difficult to identify for both the teacher and learner. Often opportunities develop only a superficial level of understanding, for example, the children might discuss that it is difficult to move a supermarket trolley because it is full of shopping. Miming that movement can bring the activity alive and then the idea can be explored by asking what would happen if you had to move it on different surfaces, e.g. sand or mud. Miming movement can provide a very useful and engaging series of visual images for teachers and learners to reflect deeply about what is happening, why and can it be explained?

Miming movement can be used in different ways to:

- elicit what children know;

- enable them to enact (and experiment with) their own ideas and understandings;

- 'see' others' views/understandings and reflect to 'improve' or hone their own; and

- show what they have learned at the end of a topic.

For example children could imagine how they might walk through a bowl full of chocolate. Some questions to consider might be: *How will changing the material that you walk on affect how you move?*; *Is it more difficult to lift your foot?*; *If it is sticky would it slow you down or allow you to walk faster?* From a teaching perspective, the teacher or peers can see immediately each child's understanding of that chocolate or other material in the bowl. For example, some children will walk normally, some will swim, others will wade – each way of moving 'tells' the teacher about the child's idea of chocolate. Learning can then be developed further by asking '*What would happen if the bowl became hotter or cooler – how would that affect the way you walk and why?*' If the teacher says 'It is getting colder!' the children's movement may change depending on their understanding of what will happen to the chocolate as it cools. Some will move slower and slower until they are stuck, others may not be sure what to do. Each of these images allows the teacher to identify children's understanding. This can then act as a spring board for investigation to find out more about the properties of chocolate. An opportunity to repeat the miming movement allows the learners to embed their new learning and for their progress in the understanding of the concept to be seen. This technique can be linked with 'freeze frame' (Chapter 6) where children are asked to freeze and the teacher or peers can ask questions such as '*I notice that you seem to be moving slower, can you tell me why?*' This gives the opportunity for the children to practise describing and explaining their ideas and has proved useful in promoting and developing the accurate use of scientific vocabulary and consolidating their understanding of scientific concepts.

Using the miming movement convention

Theme 1: The animal world

The class can be divided into groups of three or four and asked to mime how frogspawn changes into a frog. The groups can be challenged to choose a significant moment (or even two or three, if older children) and to *freeze* this moment. This can then provide the opportunity to explore the group's understanding. They can be asked: *Where are you?*; *How big are you at the moment?*; *What can you see?*; *Are you alone?*; *What might happen next?*; *What are you doing?* After several groups have shown their different mimes, the class can be asked: *What questions did the activity raise?*; *Were there any aspects of the tadpole's life you were not sure of?* Questions that arise can be noted on the white board. Through discussion the class can decide how to answer questions such as, for example: *When do gills disappear?*; *When do legs appear?*; *When is plant food no longer enough?* This can then inform what information is needed to complete the mimed movements. Watching a video clip of the life cycle or making observations over time of frogspawn developing into tadpoles can then become a focused activity to find answers to children's questions. The children can then be asked to rehearse their original mimes again, but consider (in light of additional information) how they might change what they did. Two sequential mimes (the first and the more informed) could then be practised and some performed for the whole class. Reflective discussion sharing how the mimes were improved could highlight when changes occur in the frog life cycle, e.g. when legs emerge, when gills disappear, when diet changes from eating only vegetation to include invertebrates too.

Development of skills and understanding

Miming the changes that occur when frogspawn and tadpoles develop into frogs gave children the opportunity to activate prior understandings and reflect on how change happens when creatures grow. Miming how metamorphosis arose resulted in careful reflection because the children had to think about what to do with their bodies in order to mimic the changes. They came up with questions, such as: *Do the front legs come before the back legs?*; *When do the external gills disappear?*; *When do they change what they feed on?*; *When do they stop just swimming?* These questions really focused their thinking when watching the video clip. They were then able to answer their own questions, which generated motivation because understanding *what happens* was more relevant to them. Freeze framing and finding out the children's thinking by asking questions of the 'frozen' moments enabled the children to consider what it is like to be a tadpole and the behaviours of these animals, i.e. the fact that they are often together when they hatch but become more solitary as they develop into frogs. Returning to the video and then revising their mime enabled them to deepen and consolidate their understanding and to illustrate a more detailed appreciation of the frog life cycle, developed from their own initial ideas. Some teachers used the miming movement strategy to develop children's understanding of how different animals move. When children mimed the movement of creatures found on the seashore, e.g. blenny (a fish), starfish, crab and anemone it was clear that they understood that a blenny can move itself forward using the fins at the front of its body, that crabs move sideways and that the clawed limbs are not involved in this movement and that anemones open and close. Freeze framing allowed the depth of understanding to be seen when the children described the fact that the anemones opened when the tide came in and closed when the tide went out. It also raised discussion as to which way up a starfish 'sat' as the child lay on their back. Miming how other animals moved, e.g. snails, crocodile and giraffe opened up how difficult it was for the children to move in certain ways. This prompted the children to ask questions such as: *Why does a snail have no legs?*; *Why is a crocodile close to the ground?*; *Why is a giraffe so tall?* Along with more general questions such as *Why are some animals fast and some slow?* Other teachers used the miming technique to explore animal behaviour, e.g. how the Emperor penguins look after their eggs. Again it enabled the children to raise rich questions and to consider *Why is it more difficult for humans to transfer the egg than penguins in the Antarctic?*, prompting curiosity as to how penguin feet differ from human feet and what it was about penguin feet that made it easier for them to hold the egg. Miming proved a useful technique to develop deeper interest, curiosity and understanding of animal life through raising rich scientific questions. Quotes from children included 'We liked acting out and making a mime', 'It's fun because you can use your imagination and helps you "feel" and "move" like something else or somebody else, so you get to learn stuff.'

Theme 2: Sports

The children can be given a number of cards with different sporting activities on, e.g. football, javelin, swimming, marathon running, rowing. They can then be asked to mime the movements that they would do if taking part in that sport. Other children can watch and describe what they see and explain what they think the movements indicate about the sport that is being mimed (See Figure 5.1). For example, children might bend down and mime lifting something up – what do the movements say about the shape and mass of the object they are lifting? By listening to the (deductive) discussion (and suggestions from each watching group) the children can gradually build up a picture of what the sport might be. After each group has offered their interpretations, the children could return to their groups to reflect, 'guess' or propose what the sport might be

Figure 5.1 Showing children dragging the hammer or perhaps the shot (for athletics)

with reasons for their views. When all the ideas have been shared the miming group can explain to the class what they have been enacting.

Teachers have reported that they were amazed when they found out their year threes were expert 'fencers' or 'anglers' and even 'horse riders'! Asking the children to first act out how they might play or carry out their sport is a good warm-up exercise. Then, giving them a choice of (unknown) words (selected from downturned cards, e.g. Table 5.1), they have to consider what clothing they might wear to play their sport and then practise acting out how they would put the clothing on.

TABLE 5.1 Cards that can be copied and then randomly selected by children to provide the focus for their enactments

Sport clothing	Material
Helmet	Stone
Shoes	Ice
Socks	Wood
Gloves	Elastic
Knee protectors	Cotton wool
Tracksuit	Tin foil
Elbow protectors	Paper

Children can be encouraged to be more independent by developing their own cards for the sports.

Extending learning

This activity can be extended further by having a second set of cards with different sponsors e.g. Rowntree's jelly, Cadbury's chocolate, Ikea wood. The children can be invited to take a second card that says who has sponsored the building of the sports equipment. The children then need to think about their sports equipment now made from jelly, chocolate or wood! The groups can be asked to mime their sport with their *new* equipment. The other children can be invited to watch carefully and then describe: *What do they see now?*; *How have the movements changed?*; *What does that tell them about the material?*; *Is it heavy or light, flexible or rigid?*; *What difference is the material making to the sport?*; *What do they think the sponsor's material is?*; *What was it about the movements that made them think this?*

Sports taking place in different climates (countries): Learning can be extended even further by asking the children to imagine that the Olympics are taking place in a very hot/very cold country. *How will that effect the equipment (the football, the rowing boat, their swimsuits)?* Can they mime what playing the sport will be like with their new equipment in a very hot or very cold country?

Development of skills and understanding

This approach can be applied to a wide range of scientific concepts; changing state, electrical circuits, growing organisms, properties of materials, etc. Having the children mime how they see things changing, working or moving can illustrate to others (and the teacher) their interpretations of scientific concepts.

Teachers' reflection

When teachers tried out miming movement to explore different sports the response was very positive. Children from all backgrounds and abilities were eager to participate and remained highly motivated. It allowed all involved to gain understanding of the wide variety of sports that the children were aware of and show what they did outside school. Using the 'Describe what you see' and 'What does that tell you?' approach allowed the children to practise the skill of considering information/what is presented and also opened up their thinking to recognise that there could be a range of possible answers to a question. It also helped them to consider how deductions from *evidence* can help to shape and develop an idea. For example, when miming fielding, netball or a throwing event in athletics, learners were able to use the *evidence* of the actions to come up with the idea that something was thrown or caught. Reflecting further, they can then consider if it is something heavy or light (shot-put or cricket ball), long or small (javelin or tennis ball) that has been thrown. The miming also activated other aspects of their science knowledge. For example, when learners mimed running, the speed of the running and the facial expressions (and bodily actions) could convey that it was a longer race because people became sweaty and tired (dragging limbs, etc.). When miming swimming, the opening and closing of the mouth (at a lower or higher position) provides evidence that breathing needs controlling and it was not possible to breathe underwater. Reflective discussion considering how different kinds of body actions (such as throwing or running) can be related to gravity, air resistance or even friction can really engage the children in realising why science is important in everyday life. Miming the sports activity using different fabrics also unveiled children's ideas about the properties of materials. Children miming rowing in a chocolate boat in a hot country were seen to lick their fingers and then gradually fall into the water as the chocolate melted. When children mimed playing archery one child was seen picking up the bow, another was the arrow and showed the force as they hit the third child, enacting hitting the target. When the *equipment* was made of rock the children's understanding was clear as they struggled to pick up the 'heavy' arrow, the child enacting the 'heavier' arrow then knocked over the target showing understanding of the greater force involved. Miming also highlighted a lack of experience of materials: when asked to mime swimming in a sponge swimsuit, one learner mimed jumping into the water and swimming normally – when asked what difference it would make they felt it would not make any difference. Another illustrated how to do the crawl one-handed, as the other held the costume to her body. She explained that her sponge swimsuit absorbed the water, became heavier and looser around her body, so she had to clasp it tightly so it didn't stretch too much and fall off!

Miming, therefore, can elicit a range of ideas, illustrating to the teacher the current conceptions that the children hold. This can help teachers to plan learning experiences that enable children to develop their understanding of how that material (sponge) behaves in water. The 'talk' as children prepare and rehearse their mimes can also inform teachers about their understanding(s). Adopting the freeze frame approach, pausing the mime part-way through, can also be used creatively to invite children to think about and discuss *What could happen next?* or *What does it show?* Explaining their ideas after freeze framing can support better, more effective and appropriate use of scientific vocabulary to describe and explain what could happen with different materials.

Theme 3: Food

i. Food for energy

Divide the children into groups of three or four. Ask the children or let them choose an activity that they are familiar with, e.g. either playing tag or playing on the computer. Ask them to mime that movement and then ask them: *What can they see?*; *What are they doing?*; *Which parts of the body are they using?*; *How much energy does it take?*; *What do they think the energy is used for?*; *Where do they think they get their energy from?*; *What foods might they have if they run out of energy?*; *Can they continue to play forever?*; *Why/why not?*

Extending thinking further

Learning can be extended further by giving the children a card of what they can eat. Tell the children they need to imagine that they can only eat this type of food. The groups can then be asked to mime the effects of eating only one kind of food. They could show how their growth and energy levels, health or illness might alter after eating only this food for a day, for a week, or for a year! They could be encouraged the think about: *How active are they?*; *Is it easier or harder to move?*; *How do they feel? Why?*; *What could they do to make them feel better?*; *Which foods might they need more or less of?*

Development of skills and understanding

Miming movement of different activities after eating only one type of food developed children's understanding of what would happen through discussion of what they think might happen before carrying out their mime. Children found it easy to mime what would happen if they ate just sweets probably due to discussion with adults about too many sweets making you sick. The effects of eating too many vegetables would make you feel bloated and full and result in more wind! The activity allowed children to see the importance of balancing what you eat over a period of time. For example eating sweets only for one day had little effect but for a week it makes a difference. For a year was more difficult with young children, but with children with more understanding about how the foods are used in the body they were able to see the longer term effects on teeth and growth.

ii. Source of food

Another way of using miming movement to give a group of children (three or four children) a raw food and food in its processed form, e.g. potato and potato smiley face, picture of a bullock and a beef burger, butter bean and tin of baked beans, fish and fish finger. Encourage them to read the labels for clues. Some children may need a list of ingredients or the ingredients themselves. Ask the children to discuss, rehearse and then mime how they think the food is turned into its 'produced' form. Ask the remaining children to say what they observe and what they think is happening. *What was surprising to the children? Were there any ingredients that they did not expect to see? Does anything happen that they did not expect?*

Development of skills and understanding

Miming their ideas about how food is produced raised a lot of discussion. There is debate about how much young children should understand about where their food comes from. Children will be intrigued to know what is added to the food as it is processed and this can contribute to their decisions on healthy eating. Some teachers may not want to use examples of beef burgers until their children are older. It was interesting to see that killing fish for fish fingers was seen as more acceptable that killing bullocks for beef burgers – and that is a decision for each teacher.

Theme 4: Exploration

Another scenario where miming movement that worked well was exploration. Ask the children to imagine they have just arrived on a desert island. The drama technique 'mind movies' (Chapter 8) can support this activity. Ask the children: *How might they move in this place?*; *Would they move more slowly or more quickly?*; *How might our movement change if we were walking uphill?*; *How might we move over different terrains?* Ask the children to mime this movement over different terrains, e.g. up a hill, along a sandy beach, through thick mud. *Is it harder/ easier? Are they moving faster or slower? What happens if they move down the hill?* Ask the children to freeze and ask questions to probe their understanding: *What is happening to you?*; *Why are you moving in this way?*

Extending thinking

The children could be introduced to the idea of moving a heavy trunk across the island. They can be told that the trunk has been washed up on the shoreline and that the trunk has many things in that will help them to survive. They could be told they need to move it to the other side of the island where there is water, and where it is safer or the terrain is better to build a shelter. In groups of four, the children are challenged to move the heavy trunk. *How heavy does it feel? What will you do to move it?* Any ideas that do not involve moving the box can be challenged, e.g. you cannot unpack it as it is locked. The activity can be extended even further by giving each group an unknown terrain, e.g. sandy beach, winding path, up a hill, through a swamp. The children can be encouraged to keep

Figure 5.2 A moment-in-a-mime that was developed to illustrate the children's view of germination

the terrain known to their group alone. They can be asked to mime moving it along through the given terrain. *What can the children see? What does that tell them about the terrain the group is moving the box over? What terrain do the children think it is and why?*

Development of skills and understanding

This technique can uncover children's understanding of the forces needed to move their bodies and the effect different materials could have on moving. It highlighted the children's lack of experiences such as walking in sand, mud and on logs. When moving the box over different materials some children related it to their prior knowledge of moving a pram on the beach on holiday. The strategy also developed children's problem solving skills in that the children thought of ways to overcome the difficulties different scenarios posed when moving the box. The technique of considering different contexts (or situations) encouraged exploration of distinct possibilities about how to control the movement of the box. Questions such as the following arose through applying this particular drama task in the classroom: *What would happen if you had more people at the front than at the back?; What is making it easy or hard to move?; How could you do it more safely?; What could you use to help you?; How do you push?; What helps you push?; Why is it going faster/slower?; What did you do to make it go faster/slower/ change direction?; What did you do to . . . make it move? . . . to get around that?; Did you all push at the same time?; What other heavy things have you pushed or pulled? Was it the same?; What helped?; and What would happen if you pushed it at the top/ bottom?* Considering such questions challenged and developed children's thinking about how pushes and pulls can affect how something moves.

Reflections from the classroom

One of the fascinating outcomes of the drama project is how quickly it becomes clear the assumptions that we make about what learners understand. For example, when children are asked to be a piece of chocolate many interesting depictions are communicated. As adults, (teachers of science) we might expect a solid to be represented as a 'block or rectangle'. When children show what they

Figure 5.3 Miming the forces applied to toys, e.g. the push required to close the jack-in-the-box, as depicted here

think chocolate is, some lie in straight lines, others crouch in an arc or form a circle, others sit regimented in lines. These varied interpretations conveyed by the children initiate intrigue. Why do they 'show' a solid the way they have? Asking children what they are intending to show, they will say 'matchmakers', a 'chocolate orange', or just a 'bar of chocolate'. When asked to mime what will happen if they are left on the window sill on a sunny day the learners visibly change their shape, becoming more fluid and eventually flattening out on the floor. This allows us to 'see' their thinking. Freeze framing (that is, asking them to *pause* their mime) can enhance the learning by asking the children *What are you showing? Why are you moving as you are? When will you stop moving?* Teachers found the miming movement technique illuminating in that it uncovered a wide range of children's ideas, for example, the way they perceived germination (Figure 5.2) and forces involved in making a toy move (Figure 5.3) if gravity were halved or doubled. What was also interesting was that the children drew on life experiences to support miming the movements, e.g. walking in mud, on sand, on stones, across logs, etc. Teachers also expressed that children needed to be given several opportunities to develop this technique to gain confidence and that working in groups also supported this. Children initially found it embarrassing to work individually but became more confident over time.

6

Freeze frame and tableau

Introduction to the approach

Freeze frame

Freeze frame provides an opportunity to generate 'a–moment–in–time' (often of a continuous process), which can be frozen and held like a three-dimensional photograph. The technique involves inviting individuals or groups to act out a phenomenon, then on hearing an agreed cue or sign, e.g. freeze/clap the group/individual stops and holds their position. All groups can be asked to 'freeze' simultaneously, but then in turn (like a carousel) the class can relax to look at each reformed 'still' (group or individual). This can enable everyone to see each other's frozen pose and reflect on what was happening at that moment. Such an approach can provide opportunities to contemplate, explore and examine one or several instances (in a frog's life; in the water cycle; in the growth of a plant; in the acceleration of a car down a hill; in the movement of earth around the sun). Discussion about the science they each convey can promote a greater depth of understanding. This strategy can be highly effective when used in conjunction with miming movement, modelling and spontaneous role play.

Examination and exploration of the 'frozen moment' is a valuable way of eliciting children's ideas and expanding their understanding of what is happening in the moment. For example, a frozen moment in the frog's life cycle can, through questioning, result in children considering (in role as a tadpole) broader aspects of the frog's life-cycle. Questions that arise could include: *What can they see around them?*; *What is their environment like?*; *Are they alone?*; *Can they see any food?* For older children, they might consider: *How do they move?*; *How do they feed?*; *How do they get oxygen?* These kinds of questions could be posed by the teacher, but often they arise as a result of the children thinking through how they can demonstrate the kinds of things a tadpole does, i.e. show how it moves and grows. This technique can provide a very accurate picture of children's understanding.

Tableau

The tableau technique is similar to freeze frame, in that it is a 'still representation', but it is used to explore a single expression of an idea, concept or process rather than a 'moment in time'. The tableau may, for example, illustrate 'working scientifically' or 'rocks' or 'pollination'. In this way tableaux can be used to help children to develop a greater understanding of the breadth of a concept or process. For example, children may build up a tableau about rocks. Some might consider depicting the properties of the rocks, others might focus on what they might be used for, and when groups review the tableaux they gain all these further ideas in a memorable way. The technique can also be used to develop understanding of how scientists work. By listening to the stories of scientists (Chapter 9 and Appendices), the children can use the technique to build up a picture of the skills, attitudes, dispositions and emotions that a scientist might demonstrate. The children act out a particular skill, attitude or emotion they think a scientist has. A (whole class) tableau (similar to Figure 6.1) can then be built up. Each child, having created a pose, adds this to the group tableau.

Figure 6.1 Tableau of Lavoisier, a French scientist who investigated the movement of gasses (each child is conveying a different trait of the scientist)

Others can then observe the frozen picture and consider: *What can they see?*; *What does that tell them about that scientist?* These suggestions can be discussed so that the children then have a clear idea of the dispositions and skills that are needed to work as a scientist.

A teacher reflected on using a monologue (Chapter 9) to start a lesson. She used the Lavoisier one (see Appendix 1), and encouraged the children to think about the 'facts' they learned about him, the inferences they could make about him and the things that they imagined about him. They discussed how he changed the way that science was done in the 18th century (over 300 years ago), that he repeated his measurements to improve the accuracy of his findings and that he also carried out his science in Paris, where he performed fantastic public demonstrations to communicate his ideas. In the tableau (Figure 6.1), the children are conveying 'in thought', 'writing things down', 'being a performer' and 'having ideas'. Most teachers report that the monologue and tableau are good (sequential) techniques to use because all the different elements of doing science as well as the characteristics of a good scientist are made more obvious for the children.

Theme: Exploration

There are many ways to use these techniques of freeze frame and tableau. The children can be acting out a particular role of a scientist, e.g. a plant hunter. By freezing a moment in their role play the feelings, attitudes and skills of the scientist can be explored: *What can you see?*; *Why is that interesting to you?*; *What will you do?*; *How do you feel?*; *Who will be interested?*; *What equipment have you got?*; *How will you use it?*; *Some people think . . . do you agree?*; *How will you record your findings?* This might prompt the children to consider how to explore, draw and research a plant they have found using similar skills to a scientist. A more in-depth look at a botanist could be gained by studying the life story of a scientist such as Marianne North (a famous Victorian plant hunter). After listening to a monologue the children might ask: *What do we know about this person?*; *What do we think we know?*; *What do we imagine about this person from what we know?* Words and phrases to answer these three questions can be captured in various ways, e.g. using a voice recorder, written on speech bubbles, etc. to then be reflected on at length. The children can then be asked to form a circle and act out the words or phrases that describe aspects of her character or the way she behaved. They can be asked to individually prepare a frozen depiction of one of the words or phrases that they think represent the characteristics of this scientist (see Figure 6.2). Following this, children can choose a point at which they want to add their freeze frame to the growing whole-class-tableau. They could do this by simply walking into a space in the room and holding their freeze-frame position or by connecting with one of the other freeze frames, e.g. touching another child's shoulder. Once the tableau is built up children can reflect on it by either walking around it or photographing it. As a focused discussion, children could have the opportunity to share their interpretations of the frozen pictures and consider: *What do they see or interpret from the frozen statues?*; *What does that convey about the scientist?*

Figure 6.2 A child freeze framing Marianne North as an observer and artist

Once the children are more experienced in this approach they can produce smaller tableaux and alternately walk around each other's to build up a picture of the skills, attitudes and emotions of this scientist. To extend this activity further they could compare concepts associated with the scientist or the abilities that they have portrayed in their work by comparing tableaux – alternately moving into and out of position on a cue.

Freeze frame can also be used to extend spontaneous role play (Chapter 3) by enabling the exploration and examination of the thoughts and feelings of individuals in different roles. For example, a plant hunter might find a unique plant – he/she might want to decide whether to dig the plant up to take it back to find out more about it. People in a range of different roles within the role play might have different views. Freeze framing would allow the person to share their viewpoint and reasoning. The children might be building a shelter (see Chapter 3) and then be asked, *What would you need to do if it rains heavily or there are strong winds?* Children can be asked to freeze frame as they are miming and at the *frozen* moment, be asked: *What is happening?*; *What is the wind doing?*; *How do you feel?*; *How is this affecting what you are doing?*; *Is it more difficult/less difficult? Why?*; *What will you do?*; *How will this help?*

The technique supports the drama technique of modelling. The children can work in groups of four to six. The children can be asked to use their bodies to represent or 'model' a tree. Freeze frame can then be used to examine the different parts of the tree. *What are they? What do they do? Why are they important?* Other groups can walk around the freeze frame and consider *Which species of tree do you think these are and why?*

It is then possible to use 'thought tapping'. This involves asking questions of individuals that make up the tree. Through this it is possible to elicit the children's ideas on why they decided to organise themselves and take the shape they did: *I notice you have your arms spread out? Can you tell me why you decided to do this?* (see Figure 6.3). Children can also be asked why they (as the part they are depicting) are important to the tree.

Questions might include: *I notice you have one leg bent – can you tell me why?*; *I notice that you have joined your hands – can you explain why you did this?*; *Do trees' branches ever join?* Connections between their shapes (see Figure 6.4; 6.5) can be highlighted in reflective discussion, and suggestions or questions about how their models are similar or different to trees outside is helpful.

Development of skills and understanding

Freeze frame is particularly useful in eliciting children's ideas and then using them as a stimulus for the next step in learning. Children's ideas about trees can be built on by going outside and considering how trees are differently shaped, where they grow, how they differ to shrubs and other flowering plants, etc.

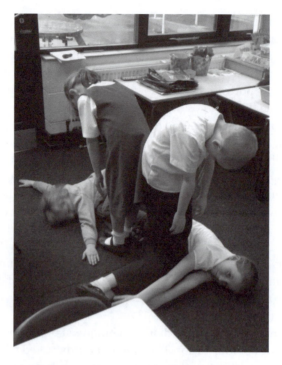

Figure 6.3 Children freeze frame the form of a weeping willow tree

Figure 6.4 Another depiction of a pine tree

Figure 6.5 A more two-dimensional enactment of a tree

Inviting the children to morph into different kinds of plants (with different trunks, stems, leaves, branches, flowers, etc) can encourage them to develop the use of scientific vocabulary in describing and explaining what they are meant to be.

The tableau technique can support children in considering evidence and drawing conclusions. Observing how groups organise themselves and then interpreting what they are depicting is an approach whereby the children consider evidence to develop ideas about *What could it be?* Making connections with other things they already know about can make learning more relevant, and then acting the ideas out can help them to become more memorable.

Theme: Sports

In this theme, pairs of children can be given sets of cards of various nouns related to sports equipment, e.g. swimming trunks, cycle helmet, swimming

hat, shorts, socks, leotard, etc. Each pair selects one card. They then mime putting on that item of clothing. They can be asked to choose from a second set of
'material' cards, e.g. wool, wood, rock, paper, rubber, sponge. The children are
then asked to mime (see miming movement chapter) putting the item of clothing on made of this new material and given the cue to freeze or choose a significant point at which to freeze. That moment can then be explored by asking
the children to describe how the material acts and behaves (e.g. restricts their
movements or keeps them warm by insulating them). Children from other
groups might also choose an interesting moment to freeze and tap the miming
person to ask them questions.

Children involved in using mind movies to imagine sports taking place
when sponsored by confectionary companies is a fun way to develop ideas
about different materials that might be used in sport. Children could be told
everything was made of a particular kind of sweet, such as jelly or chocolate. Different groups of children could be asked to mime their sport when
everything was made of jelly, chocolate or ice cream. The whole *scene* can be
frozen and observers asked: *What do they notice?*; *What does that tell them about
the sponsored material?*; *What questions might they ask?*; *Is it . . . heavy/light? . . .*

Figure 6.6 Children sprinting in a cold place where everything has turned to ice

flexible/rigid?; *What might happen if they put the object into water?*; *What difference does it make to the sport?*; *What do they think the sponsor material is?* When the scene is transported to a hotter or colder location, again freeze frame can support children to explore the differences in the scene by choosing a significant moment, for example, when the chocolate boat they are rowing begins to melt, again the children can be prompted to think about: *What is happening? Why?*; *What will you do?*; *How will you get to shore?*; *Could you swim?*, prompting thinking about the properties of chocolate and the effects of increasing temperature. Another scenario could be the athletics track freezing over (Figure 6.6).

Development of skills and understanding

The freeze frame is particularly useful to explore children's thinking. With careful questioning the technique supports children to consider questions that they might not have thought of and it can even prompt problem solving. Consider, for example, exploring ideas about friction by asking the children to enact and freeze at various points playing football on a chocolate, ice or jelly pitch. Sharing 'frozen' moments during running, passing the ball or goal scoring can illustrate a wide range of ideas that children hold about forces, mass and friction. This can uncover disparities, gaps or misunderstanding in children's thinking. In terms of the properties of chocolate, showing how they change what they do as it melts, how runny (and slippery) they think it might be and how they may lose grip as friction decreases, all contributes to appreciating the extent of the children's understanding. Because the children have to answer questions and explain their thinking, this approach is useful for developing the use and application of scientific vocabulary, as well as talking and explaining ideas.

Theme: Food

In the theme of food, children can be asked to *freeze* three significant moments from their modelling of the production process of various foods, e.g. fish finger; catching a fish, gutting the fish, mixing it with other ingredients. Children can be asked what they can see and what it reveals to them about the moment. The children modelling can be asked: *What are you doing?*; *How do you feel?*; *How many fish have you used?*; *What are you adding to the mixture?*; *Would you eat it yourself? Why? Why not?* Children can also use freeze frame to explore moments over time when they are miming eating the same foods, for example, for one day, one month or one year. *How do they feel? How has this changed? What affect has it had on their body?* Questions can be used to delve deeper depending on the level of knowledge of the children: *How has it affected your teeth?*, etc.

Figure 6.7 Freeze framing how a vegetable grows (broccoli)

The technique can be used to identify significant moments in the development of a plant, for example, the growth of a tomato plant or broccoli (Figure 6.7). Children can produce a frozen image of what they consider to be an important moment. This can then be a focus for discussion: *What could the image reveal?*; *What could the poses tell us about the plant?* Alternatively the children in the pose can be thought tapped and questioned: *What can you see?*; *Are you underground or above? Why?*; *How do you grow?*; *What is next to you?*; *Are you in a bunch or on your own?*; *Do you grow on the stem/the root?*; *Where do you get your food and water from?*; *What will happen to you next?* Freeze frame can also be used to identify significant moments when the children are using the miming movement technique. When considering chocolate the children can be asked to mime what might happen if they were on a sunny windowsill (Figure 6.8) or in a fridge. The moment can be frozen and then the children asked: *What is happening to you?*; *How are you changing?*; *What is different?*; *What is the same?*; *Why are you changing?*; *What is causing the change?*

The freeze frame technique can also be used to investigate significant moments when children are carrying out a spontaneous role play, for example,

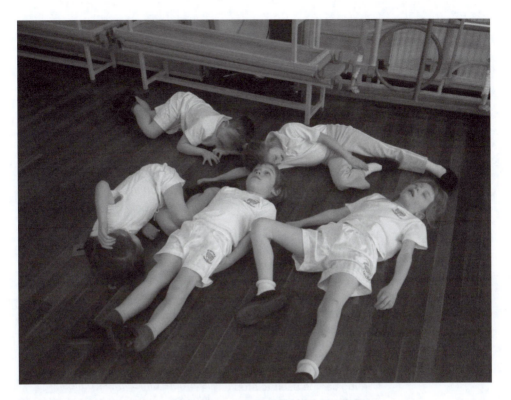

Figure 6.8 Children modelling and freezing a key moment when chocolate melts

when children are in role as different members of a family buying food in a supermarket. If the different family members have different needs, e.g. one is a toddler, another is allergic to peanuts, another does not like meat, freeze framing extends the activity set up in 'spontaneous role play (Chapter 3) by allowing the thinking and feelings of particular characters to be explored: *Which food do you want to choose and why?*; *Would that food be the choice of others in the group? Why/why not?*; *If you choose that food, how might the others feel?*

Theme: Desert island

The following tables indicate how freeze frame can be used in conjunction with other drama techniques within the themes of desert island (Table 6.1) and toys (Table 6.2).

Within the desert island theme, freeze frame can be used to enhance learning with other drama techniques (see Table 6.1).

TABLE 6.1 Using freeze frame to teach about life (or survival) on a desert island

Drama technique	Scenario	Questions to ask
Spontaneous role play	Children role play designing a shelter to meet the needs of a varied group of castaways, e.g. one who feels the cold, one who is frightened of creepy crawlies and one who needs to stay out of the sun.	How are you making the shelter comfortable for everyone?
		How will it keep bugs out?
		How will that work?
		Will it keep all bugs out? Why/why not?
	Freeze framing can draw out the thinking of individual members of the group.	How will you make it darker/lighter?
		Is it waterproof?
	They can then be given additional scenarios, e.g. weather such as heavy rain or strong winds.	How have you made it waterproof?
		Will it be warm?
		What have you done to make it warm?
	Children can be asked to mime how they would change their shelter (to cope with different forces applied from the wind) and absorbency of water (from the rain). Freeze framing can be used to stop the mime at any point to request their explanations (of their actions).	What is happening?
		What is the wind doing?
		How do you feel?
		How is this affecting what you are doing?
		Is it more difficult/less difficult? Why?
		What will you do? How will this help?
		What can you feel?
Miming movement	Children role play moving a heavy box. Freeze framing can be used to stop the mime at any point to request their explanations (of their actions).	What are you doing?
		Are you pushing or pulling?
		Is everyone pushing?
		Is it easy or hard to push? Why?
		Let's think how heavy this box is. Would it be that easy to move?
		How might you change your movement?
		Is it easy or hard to pull?
		What is making it harder?
	Children can be asked to mime moving the heavy box over different terrains, e.g. up a hill, down a hill, on a sandy beach, through a group of trees.	How do you feel?
		Is it easy or hard?
		What did you have to do to move it?
		Was it a push or a pull?
		Is it always a push or a pull?

Freeze framing can be used to stop the mime at any point to request their explanations (of their actions).

What is happening?

How will you stop/turn the box?

Is it safe?

How can you make it safe?

Does it matter where people stand?

What do they need to be careful of?

Theme: Toys

TABLE 6.2 Using freeze frame to teach about toys

Drama technique	Scenario	Questions to ask
Linking to William Harbutt (inventor of plasticine – Appendix 18) Miming movement of plasticine ball	What will happen to a ball of plasticine when it is dropped: ■ on the floor ■ into a bucket of water ■ into a bucket of syrup? Ask the children/a child to freeze frame.	Of other children when they examine the freeze-frame: *What can you see?* *What does the freeze frame tell you about what is happening/has happened to the plasticine?* *Is it floating/sinking? Why?* Of children in the freeze frame: *Can you tell me your thinking?* *I notice that your shape has changed – why?* *Is this what really happens?* *How can we find out?*[1]
Mini-historical play (Chapter 9) with children working scientifically like William Harbutt	Investigating making dough.	Of other children when they examine the freeze frame: *What do you think they are doing?* *What do you think they are thinking?* *What skills are they using?* Of children in the freeze frame: *What skills are you using?* *How are you feeling?* *What are you thinking?* *How are you working like William Harbutt?* *What do you think William Harbutt would do next?*

TABLE 6.2 Continued

Drama technique	Scenario	Questions to ask
Miming movement	The children explore a variety of toys. The children choose a toy they would like to be and rehearse how that toy moves, drawing on their experiences of exploring the toys. Set the scene.	Why did you choose this moment? Why is it important to you? What is happening? What causes you to move? What forces are involved? Will you continue moving? Why/why not? What if there were less gravity or less friction?
	The scene is a toy shop at night. Tell the children that the toys are still so that they need to be still. Tell the children that when the clock strikes midnight they (the toys) will begin to move. As the children move, they could be asked to freeze a particular moment they feel is important in showing how a toy works.	

1 An alternate approach, using drama to 'set up' an investigation.

Development of skills and understanding

Freeze framing has proved particularly useful to explore the development of children's thinking. It provides rich scientific contexts for children to practise using scientific vocabulary. It is also a rapid, insightful technique to assess the success of teaching particular concepts.

Reflections from the classroom

Tableau and freeze frame are useful ways of encouraging children to empathise with a real scientist. Many children commented that after presenting a tableaux depicting scientists' lives, they began to understand the complex processes that result in a discovery or an invention. After creating tableaux for several scientists, they also began to realise that some characteristics are quite common between them. They began to understand that a scientist can take a very long time to make a breakthrough, or that they can happen by accident; there is more appreciation that not all scientific outcomes arise in a planned, premeditated way. The children also found that when working with their own experiments they could draw parallels between themselves and characteristics of the scientists that they learned about. For example, through a tableau of Harbutt (and then making their own modelling clay), children reflected, 'We have had to try lots of different times before we got a really good dough, like William Harbutt did' (year five class, North Staffordshire school).

The freeze frame element is also very useful, particularly when children's mime or actions aren't clear, as they can be tapped and asked, *What do you mean?* As a follow on from a tableau or freeze frame, children (or the teacher) could choose to *hot seat* (Chapter 4) certain people in the freeze frame and ask further questions about what is happening or may have happened.

7

Modelling

Introduction to the approach

This approach is designed to encourage the children to physically enact their ideas and represent understandings using their bodies. They should be encouraged to change their shape, sounds and movements to (re)create as accurate a reproduction of a concept, such as the structure of a tree, an electrical circuit or the floating and sinking of different objects in water, as possible. Reflective discussion and/or further suggestions about 'what else' may be missing or forgotten can inform a *revised* enactment. Children asked to model an electrical circuit may, for example, stand in a circle, hands by their sides, as one child runs around the outside of the circle representing 'a moving electron'. There are a number of flaws with this model, so reflective discussion would be important to help the children to realise that electrons cannot travel through a circuit without 'connections', and there needs to be a power source and a switch (determining the direction of movement of the electricity). It is also important that the children appreciate that electricity will not flow through an incomplete circuit. So a circle of upright bodies with an orbiting runner is a physical model that can be reflectively improved to become a more accurate depiction of a circuit.

The children can engage in modelling, individually as well as in groups. When working in groups, there can be a high level of collaboration through discussion and decision-making about how to act out their understandings.

This approach can be used in a number of ways:

1. *To explore knowledge and understanding*
   To elicit what children know or think at the beginning of teaching a science topic. Providing children with the opportunity to 'show' what they think, understand or believe before teaching them is good practice. Knowing what 'prior' understandings they have at the beginning of a unit or theme of work informs where and how to aim subsequent lessons. Asking children, for example, to model how a plant grows from a seed, how

electricity makes a torch work or to show how a puddle is formed can illustrate a whole range of different understandings.

2. *To check knowledge and understanding*
    To review at the end of a topic or programme of work the understanding that the children have retained. This can be used to make informed judgments about how well the children have understood or remembered the concepts studied. The same requests (e.g. model how a plant grows from a seed, how electricity makes the television work or show how a puddle is formed) from the beginning of the topic can be repeated to assess how their thinking and understanding has progressed (and become more detailed).

3. *To develop and consolidate knowledge and understanding*
    The engagement with tasks (as an individual or a group) to act out what something is can enhance understanding about how that object or organism works. Consider, for example, giving groups of children an unknown seed and a large brown-coloured sheet (representing the surface of the soil) and asking them to model how might this seed develop above or below the ground. The collaborative discussion around what happens to a seed, how slowly it germinates and how it develops into a plant, and discussing when it might be in the ground or above the soil, can enliven how children 'see' and envisage what happens to growing plants.

4. *To promote prediction*
    Giving children the opportunity to show what they think might happen in an experimental situation (e.g. three similar plants, one given water every day; one given water once a week; one not given any water, or three similar small Christmas tree light bulbs, each connected to a 1.5v battery differently with two wires).

5. *For spontaneous formative assessment*
    Children engaged and actively participating in 'acting out' through drama any of their ideas and scientific understandings can provide teachers with spontaneous illustrations and depictions of their thinking at that moment in time.

Guidance to use 'modelling'

Modelling could be applied to almost anything being taught in science.

Theme: Living things (Exploration)

An obvious example in the animal and plant world is for children to enact the life cycle (or aspects of it) of living things, for example, seed germination and pollination; a penguin protecting an egg whilst the chick grows inside; the growth of a tree. Illustrations of these ideas can be purposely requested to help the teachers to see what the children understand or believe before they are taught about animals and plants. Having children work in small groups (three or four) can work better than pairs because they can 'display' more complexity through their collective actions.

Figure 7.1 shows how the teacher organised the children to work outside in the playground (with their coats on) and model aspects of the penguin's life

Figure 7.1 Huddling penguins (with coats on for insulation) in the school yard

Figure 7.2 Father transferring an egg to the mother penguin so he can go to feed

history. As a teacher, of course, you could ask them to model each of the stages (Figure 7.2; 7.3) and reflectively discuss what it means to be a penguin living in the Antarctic. The picture depicts how a teacher encouraged the children to empathise with penguin parents looking after their egg (modelled by a ball). The children can be challenged to act as the paternal penguin trying to balance the egg on their feet (as a father would need to do) to ensure it doesn't touch the icy ground, become too cold and perish. Children are likely to remember this activity because of the novelty value and the unique outdoor experience. In 'being' the penguin, the hope is that they will come to better understand

Figure 7.3 Practising balancing the model penguin 'egg' on your human (non-webbed) feet

and appreciate how a penguin is adapted (webbed feet for balancing on icy, slippery surface; male holding egg above the ground to keep it warm; thick layer of fat and feathers to insulate against cold temperatures, etc.) to live in such a cold inhospitable environment.

With a whole class, you could give different groups different aspects of a life cycle to enact and place the children in a carousel around the room and choreograph each one coming 'alive' in sequence so that the whole process, from egg, hatching, growing, developing, becoming mature, mating and laying own egg, is depicted around the classroom.

The children could be asked at any point if they have questions. What is likely to arise are queries that they (and you) do not know the answer to, for example, *When the female lays the egg how do the parents make sure if doesn't fall on the ground? Or when the penguin hatches from the egg how does it keep warm? Or how soon can the hatchling walk?*

Opportunities for reflective discussion

After each 'enactment' there are questions that really probe their scientific reasoning and understanding:

1. How did it feel to be a penguin?

2. How did you cope as a penguin at this point in your life?

3. How is the penguin's life different to yours?

4. How accurate is your enactment of the penguin's life?

These questions become an almost 'hot seating' of the children as 'experts' of their aspect of the life cycle of the penguin.

Theme: Muscles and movement

Teaching about the way bones and muscles work together to enable parts of the body (joints) to move is possible, and great fun, through this approach. The teacher can instruct the children how to model the bones and muscles in the joints, or it can be explained to the pupils (by watching a video or listening to the teacher) and then they can attempt to reproduce the movement in a small group. The collaboration required between the children to co-ordinate the sequence of movements correctly involves discussion and enactment of their understanding. As a teacher reflected, they can even enhance the movement and make noises as if they are using more effort, etc. She also shared how this could be revised to show movement when (imagining) wearing different materials, like running in paper trousers, having jelly shoes or a wearing a heavy stone helmet. Combining miming movement and modelling in this way could then enable the children to identify the short-comings of different materials (that athletes could potentially wear) and adapt their movements accordingly. Children can be invited to model the working of specific muscle groups/joints,

Figure 7.4 (a & b) Modelling different phases of knee movement

for example the knee joint (see Figure 7.4), or the elbow, demonstrating understanding of how muscles work together in pairs. One teacher explained how she had used this as an effective assessment tool; after the children had been taught how the elbow works, they had to work out and demonstrate the knee moving. As she further noted, the models were sometimes not perfect: the boy as the "foot" (in Figure 7.4 a and b) had to move the shin bone as the knee bent and straightened. Explanation about why the model wasn't quite right was also educational for the children.

Opportunities for reflective discussion

Reflective discussions can be had about why they are modelling moving in a particular way (through the combination of miming movement and modelling). Children could be paused (freeze framed) and then asked why certain movements are happening, or how their muscles feel when they are moving through treacle, which muscles are doing the work as the knee straightens and why they may need to move in a certain way if wearing paper trousers, etc.

Before the activity

It may be useful for children to research different muscles and bones, and hot seat the 'experts' before this activity, in order to elicit more scientific understanding of the muscles used when modelling.

Theme: Desert island and survival

Modelling and miming movement related to the desert island scheme (see Table 7.1) could include enacting:

a. moving an invisible heavy trunk from the sea shore through the sand, onto marshy ground and then over the rocky terrain to the cave where it can be safely opened. Emphasis on the forces required to move the trunk (pushes and pulls) that need to overcome the friction.

b. responding as different materials found on the strandline, when a magnet (force field) is encountered on the island. Children can be given objects or told that they are a faded piece of torn fabric, an old twisted metal chair leg, some frayed rope, the battered casing of a torch, etc . . . and have to respond as they think these things might behave if the island became strongly magnetic.

c. how a torch works. Having found remains of a torch on the strandline, you need to make it work to signal for help. *How does it work?* The children can be organised in small groups to act out how it works.

d.   modelling the spread of a disease that might develop, using hand cream and glitter.

How easy it is to pass on micro-organisms can be effectively demonstrated using glitter. Two volunteers rub hand cream on their hands, then glitter is sprinkled on, each child having a different colour. The rest of the class stands in a circle, and the two volunteers go round, one shaking hands with the others, and one doing high fives. After a couple of minutes, the class is stopped, and children look to see how much glitter (representing micro-organisms) has made its way onto their hands, faces (see Figure 7.5 (a & b)), etc. This can be followed up by teaching on the importance of good hand washing technique.

Theme: Food and plants

Modelling can be used to involve virtually the whole class to illustrate how something grows (see Table 7.2). This example of modelling a tree can be adapted.

The activity can be introduced to the children by asking each of the following questions in turn.

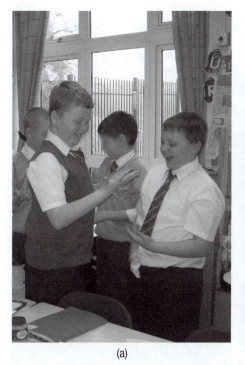
(a)

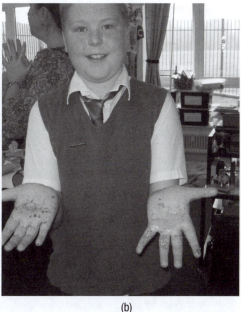
(b)

Figure 7.5 (a & b) Modelling the spread of germs (and disease)

TABLE 7.1 A summary of questions, answers and subsequent actions to model how a tree works

Teacher activity	Children's responses
Q: What does a tree need to support it and keep it standing upright and straight? Directions: three of you (taller children are best here) stand, backs to each other, hold hands in a circle and chant 'I support, I support, I support'.	A: A tree trunk or the stuff (lignin) that holds it together.
Q: Where do trees get their water from? Q: How do trees obtain this water? Directions: three more of you sit at the base of the trunk with your legs spread out (representing roots) and chant 'I absorb water, I absorb water, I absorb water'.	A: Soil. A: Through the roots.
Q: How does the water get from the roots to the leaves? Directions: two inside the trunk, face each other and hold hands, bend knees and move up and down chanting 'I move water, I move water, I move water'.	A: Through pipes inside trunk.
Q: Where does the water go?	A: Up inside the trunk (through tubes) to the leaves.
Q: Why do plants need water?	A: To keep the trunk and cells firm; for making food (photosynthesis).
Q: Where do plants make their food? Directions: three more of you stand on chair place one hand on a 'trunk' person and other out to the side and chant 'I make food, I make food, I make food'. (For older children you could ask them to say 'I produce food'.)	A: In leaves.
Q: Where does the food go that is made in the leaves? Directions: two of you stand inside the water tube (between the other two) hold hands bend knees and move up and down and chant 'I move food, I move food, I move food'. (For older children you could ask them to say 'I transport food'.)	A: Down a tube that carries it to the growing parts, like the roots.
Q: What will happen as the weather warms and we move from winter into summer?	A: More water moves up to leaves; more food is made; processes quicken.

Q: What will happen as the weather cools and we move from summer into winter?	A: Less water is needed by the leaves as they are making less food; processes slow down; leaves fall off.
Directions: lets chant how we develop as the seasons change . . . it's getting warmer . . . sunnier . . . it's becoming spring . . . and now summer . . . it is now getting colder . . . longer nights . . . less sunlight . . . it's now autumn . . . and now winter.	Chanting of the 'jobs' of each part of the tree by all the children together gradually increases speed to become very fast during the summer, then as the autumn sets in the chanting slows . . . and then becomes very slow and the leaves fall off.

The final working model of a tree will involve most of the children in the class.

Reverse modelling

This is where the teacher directs the children to model something without explaining it, and the children can be challenged to work out what it represents.

Imagine the setting described below.

The teacher asks the children to stand at least an arms-length apart. The teacher then weaves through the standing children with arms outstretched. Three different coloured (blue, white and green) tokens are scattered on the floor.

When the teacher has scattered the tokens, the children are asked to wriggle their toes to reach one of each coloured token. Anyone who does not touch a green, blue and white token then has to fall to the ground and not move again.

The children are asked to consider what has been demonstrated.

It can be interpreted as a wood (the children are the trees), the tokens represent water (blue), light (white) and nutrients (green). A lack of all three essential raw materials means the trees would die.

The teachers could repeat the modelling without giving a response to the suggestions about what it might be . . . and use different proportions of light, water and nutrients to see if the children can work out which is which.

Modelling forms of trees

The children can be asked to model trees growing in different places: the dessert (yucca); by a river (weeping willow); middle of a big deciduous wood (an old oak); or even a spruce (evergreen) Christmas tree (Figure 7.6).

Modelling changes of state with chocolate and ice-cream

The children can be asked to model how chocolate changes when it is left on the window sill on a hot, sunny day. They can then be asked to show what happens when it gets cooler as evening draws nearer.

Figure 7.6 Modelling forms of trees

Modelling forces and toys

Straightforward modelling

Modelling, in combination with miming movement, can be applied to children showing how forces work on different toys. The children can be shown contrasting toys, e.g. spinning top, clockwork toy, jack-in-the-box, etc. They can be asked to then work in groups and show how these toys work (see Figure 7.7 below) and be ready to explain how forces (pushes, pulls, twists and turns) cause or result in movements of the toys.

Enabling the children to develop their reflections about theirs and others' models of their ideas can be helped by using withdrawal (so everyone continues 'modelling' whilst one group pauses and steps aside to observe the rest of the groups). There is also the carousel technique (where each group, around the room, takes it in turn to model to the rest of the class) that can be used for others to 'see' their interpretations.

Figure 7.7 Children discussing the forces to model how 'jack-in-the-box' works

Development of scientific understanding and skills

Scientific understanding will not naturally follow a novel experience, but it will certainly help many children to remember it and connect the science to describe what they did. However, to help the children really explain the science it is likely to be even more effective if they are engaged in reflecting on what they have done, so that they can describe what they did and explain it, too. Context and timing matters to most effectively apply the drama techniques.

Reflections about reverse modelling

Figure 7.8 illustrates part of a lesson about a scientist called Rachel Carson (see also Appendix 12). She was a nature lover and she warned the public about the long-term effects of misusing pesticides. She wrote a book called silent spring and after the monologue we did this reverse modelling, and the children followed instructions. They were trees in the woods and the discs on the floor (shown in the photo) were nutrients (green), light (white) and water (blue), and if you had all three you would survive and you wouldn't shrivel. Then it was

Figure 7.8 Reverse modelling the need for nutrients, water and light for tree growth

repeated with an extra disc, which was the pollutant – the orange disc. So even if you were alive but you were polluted you wouldn't survive. We then asked the children, *What do the discs stand for?* 'This photograph depicts reverse modelling, there was full participation and it really made the children think and they were offering lots of suggestions' (year six teacher, North Staffordshire school).

Reflections from the classroom

There are various contexts that the teachers used to apply the modelling strategy. Some of these are summarised in Tables 7.2–7.5. Many teachers commented that this was a useful strategy to:

1. formatively assess children's understanding pre- and post-teaching;

2. illustrate and consolidate factual scientific ideas.

TABLE 7.2 Applying 'modelling' to an exploration theme – an example

Strategy	Description of strategy	Key learning objectives	Activities	Question starters
Modelling	Modelling is a way of physically creating a representation of an object and exploring how it works/ acts.	To explore what is needed for a torch to work through modelling.	Ask the children to get into groups of six.	What do you think . . .?
			Ask them to model the way a torch might work: *How do you think a torch might work?*; *What do you think will happen next?*; *What can you tell me about this connection?*; *Why are you facing that way?*; *What would happen if . . .?*; *Would it matter if these were in a different order? Why?*	Why do you think. . .?
		To share and develop ideas of how torches work/ (different circuits).		Is it . . . or . . .?
				Would it matter if . . .?
				Can you describe how . . .?
				How do you know?
			Thought tap different components of the circuit.	What might happen if . . .?

TABLE 7.3 Applying 'modelling' to a sports theme – an example

Strategy	Description of strategy	Key learning objectives	Activities	Question starters
Modelling	Modelling is a way of physically creating a representation of an object and exploring how it works/ acts.	To explore *what ifs* through modelling.	Using two sets of cards, one set with opposite adjectives on, the other with nouns (for clothing an athlete might wear).	What do you think the object is made from?
			Words on the cards – opposite adjectives examples: Flexible and rigid; hard and soft; wet and dry; metallic and non-metallic; magnetic and non-magnetic; shiny and dull; rough and smooth.	What makes you think. . .?
		To explore the suitability of different materials for different objects.		Is it . . . or . . .?
			A set of cards with random nouns on, e.g. sweatshirt/ training shoes/ball/stick/bat/ oar.	Can you describe the material? How do you know?
			In pairs the children select (randomly) one card from each set of cards.	What might happen if . . .?
			The children then enact the opposite words using their noun, e.g. magnetic/non magnetic training shoes.	
			The rest of the group/class observe and try to guess what the noun and opposite words are.	

TABLE 7.4 Applying 'modelling' to a food theme – an example

Strategy	Description of strategy	Key learning objectives	Activities	Question starters
Modelling	Modelling is a way of physically creating a representation of an object and exploring how it works/ acts.	To share and develop ideas on how plants grow and where food grows on plants.	Children in groups of three or four.	What do you think. . . .?
			Choose a card to find out what kind of plant you are.	What might it be?
			Children model that plant.	Why do you think. . . .?
			Tell us about the plant: *What can you see?; What plant parts can you see?; What is the stem like?; Why do think it is like that?; What are the leaves like?; What does that tell you about how the plant grows?; Does it grow . . . along the floor? . . . upright? Is it tall/small, bushy/spindly?; Would it be on its own?*	Is it . . . or . . .? Can you describe where . . .? How do you know?
			Does everyone agree?	
			Children reveal the plant they are.	
			Ask second group to demonstrate their plant.	
			How is this plant the same or different?	
			Give out five 'food' cards, e.g. tomato, apple.	
			Does anyone know what this is?; How do we know?; Where do you think it grows on the plant?; How does it grow?; Where do you think it grows from – the stem or the leaves? (Children could stick the picture card where they think they would grow from.)	
			Look at the range of places that they put the pictures: *Which do we think it is right?; Why do they think that?; How would we find out if we are right?; Would it be easy to find at this time of year?; How else might we find out?*	

TABLE 7.5 Applying 'modelling' to a toys theme – an example

Strategy	Description of strategy	Key learning objectives	Activities	Question starters
Modelling	Modelling is a way of physically creating a representation of an object and exploring how it works/acts.	To develop understanding of the influences of forces on toys and their subsequent movements.	Act these out: you are playing with your toy car at home – you want to make it move forward – what do you do?	What do you think . . .?
			Your mum picks you up from school, the car breaks down – you have to get it off the road so no-one bumps into it – what do you do?	What might it be?
			What is the difference between these two pushes?	Why do you think . . .?
			Now stroke a kitten, what force are you using? Now stroke the fur backwards – *what other force is acting?*	Is it . . . or . . .?
			Now act these out: knock down a building; pull up your socks; pull a bus. *What forces are you using?* (Big and small pushes and pulls.)	Can you describe where . . .? How do you know?
			Imagine you have a big truck – you can put Mrs Cope's rabbit in it – *how different is it to move the truck with and without the rabbit?*	
			Close your eyes – you are chewing a big toffee – *what happens? Why? What forces are being used?*	
			Imagine you are in the park on your skateboard, you are going fast – someone suddenly walks in front of you – you have to stop immediately. *What forces are at work?*	
			If you were a teenager would it make a difference? Why? (Heavier – bigger push; heavier – slower to stop.)	
			You got ready for school this morning – you put your hat on – you go outside for break. It's windy – *what will happen to your hat? What should you do? What force is moving the hat? What force is keeping it on?* (Wind = a push.)	
			The teacher stands in the centre of the room and tells the children to move quickly towards her – *What am I? –* You are being pulled towards me. (Answer – magnet.) *What are you?; What could you be?*	

8

Mind movies

Introduction

Mind movies are a way of transporting the learner to another situation (beyond the classroom). Audio or visual stimuli are used to support children to imagine themselves in different places, times or contexts. The 'scene' can be set to transport the children back (or even forward) in time, to another country (or planet) or to be someone or something else. The children are encouraged to listen, feel and look carefully at images, and can be asked questions to help them visualise what a particular place (or time or situation) might be like, e.g. through using Appendix 3a, for example, to help the children imagine life in Paris in the late 1700s or by generating a soundscape (below). Mind movies are a powerful tool to tap into children's imaginations. When asked to suggest what they hear or see children draw on their many experiences and bring ideas and suggestions that can be shared to develop a rich picture of a place, time or situation.

Guidance on using mind movies

This strategy can be used in a number of ways. An effective way to begin using it is to develop the children's skills for listening and interpreting sounds.

Developing a soundscape (a set of instructions)

- Ask the children to sit in a circle.
- Make a sound such as rubbing your hands together. Ask the child on your left to copy that sound, encouraging them to make the same sound by copying your actions. Encourage them to repeat the sound accurately using the same rhythm.

- Ask the next child in the circle to copy the sound from the first child. Encourage the children already making the sound to continue. As each child around the circle joins in, the sound or 'soundscape' is built up.

- As the sound makes its way back to the starting point in the circle, change the sound, e.g. change from rubbing your hands together to a gentle clapping, slightly louder than before. Again ask the children to stop the old sound and join in making the new sound as they hear the person next to them making the new sound. Gradually the new sound is built up around the group as the old sound is dropped. When each person has made the new sound, change the sound to a slightly louder sound, e.g. tapping on the floor. Louder and louder sounds can then be passed around the circle so that the sounds make a crescendo, then the sounds can be developed around the circle getting softer and softer.

- Encourage the children to listen carefully and then envisage what the 'soundscape' sounds like. Ask them: *What can you tell me about the sound?*; *What could it be?*; *What makes a sound like this?* These sounds often make the children think of wind and rain – children will describe storms getting louder and then dying down or moving closer or further away. An interesting twist is to ask the children to carry out the activity with their eyes closed. This allows more focused listening and sharpens their imagination. The children have to listen very carefully for the change in the sound and can be seen taking a cheeky peek or moving their ears closer to the person next to them in an effort to hear the sound better and to copy it. This technique, once mastered, allows the children to independently develop their own soundscapes (see later).

Imagining a different place

Another starting point for this convention is to use sounds and images. Children can be asked to sit in a circle and to close their eyes and listen carefully. The sounds from an audio file can then be played. When the sounds have finished, the children can be asked: *What pictures did they imagine?*; *How did they know it was that place?*; *What sounds did they hear?*; *Was there anything else they could hear?*; *Can anyone use their imagination to imagine what else might be there?* The teacher can then adjust ideas by adding information: *Well it is . . . and there are . . . but I am afraid that . . . .*; *In this place not only is there . . . but maybe there is . . . .* This allows the children to build up a rich mental image of a situation or time and provide a starting point to envisage a different place from the classroom.

Figure 8.1 Using mind movies to introduce an activity

Transporting elsewhere on a magic carpet

Many teachers have used a magic carpet technique to transport the children to places beyond the classroom. Figure 8.1 shows a class who took it in turns to 'travel on a scooter' to different places and showed how the ground might affect their journey. The children had to touch the carpet and say 'We are going to go to . . . [wherever]' and then they had to ride a scooter in that different environment. It might be riding in a desert over the sand, up a mountain, across the sea, or through the park, etc. 'It is a useful learning strategy to help immerse the children in *being* somewhere and the children really enjoy it. It's also a good way, after they've done a bit of activity, to bring them back' (year six teacher, North Staffordshire school).

Theme: Exploration

The children can be asked to close their eyes and listen carefully. The sounds of waves lapping up and gently receding on a sandy beach and the sounds of sea birds crying in the wind could depict a desert island, the sound of ice cracking and howling gales could depict an icy landscape in Antarctica. The sounds of owls hooting and foxes crying could depict a woodland at night. Play the sound and ask the children: *What can you hear?*; *What does it remind you of?*; *What kind of place might this be?*; *What do you imagine you can see/hear/feel?*; *What do you think the place looks like?*; *Do you think it is hot or cold?*; *What would it feel like to walk or run in this place?* Children can then be asked to open their eyes and be shown an image of the place to be explored. Further questions can help them to immerse themselves in a particular location or situation, such as: *What extra information does the picture give?*; *What else might be there?*; *What might be beyond what you can see in the picture?*; *How do you think you would feel if you were there?*; *Is this a place you would like to visit? Why?*

Extending learning

Mind movies can be used to extend thinking further by asking: *How could we find out more?*; *What transport might we use?* Children can also use a rug to represent a magic carpet, or a silver circle for a helicopter, which the children can either sit on individually or share with others. Once on the circles or mats, the children can be encouraged to steady the machine, maintain their balance or put on their seat belts. They can be told they are going higher and higher and that you would like them to look over the side or out of the window at the landscape below, and consider what they might see. The children can be encouraged to be creative by asking them: *What can you see?*; *Can anyone see footprints?*; *What might they be?*; *Do they look like human or animal prints?*; *How big are they?*; *If there are these animals what might they eat?*; *Where might they sleep?* The teacher can strengthen the image by adding information and by encouraging the children to reflect on the image so far, i.e.: *Can anyone see . . .?*; *Can you describe them to me?*; *So what might this tell us about this place?*; *If we can see this, what else might/must be there?*

Development of skills and understanding

The mind-movies approach has shown to be very useful to elicit children's existing knowledge. Some children empathise very accurately and insightfully when asked to imagine what it might be like to be transported to another place and could describe the smells and sounds confidently. Some children found it challenging, either to engage creatively or because they didn't have relevant prior experiences that could inform their ideas. Teachers reported that the technique helped children to make connections between places that were familiar and different locations or situations that may have similar features and sounds. It also developed possibility thinking. Children drew on their experiences of the sources of sounds they knew, but also talked of the possibilities of new causes of different sounds.

Theme: Food

The mind-movies technique can support children appreciating different places where food might be grown, e.g. rice is grown in a paddy field in

China or India. The children can be asked to imagine they are sitting on a magic carpet. They can be invited to put their seat belts on as this could be a long trip. They can be reminded to 'sit still' so that they are balanced on the flying carpets. They can then be encouraged to describe what they might see if travelling over the rice paddies of Asia. Comments and questions that could be posed might include: There are fields covered with water. *I can see lots of green shoots, what might they be?*; *There are people with circular hats. What else might we see?*; *People are planting the shoots, about one handspan apart, why do you think that is?*; *I think I can see water buffalo, what might suggest to me that's what they are? What do you think they look like?*; *It seems that they are pulling something. Can anyone describe what it might look like? What could it be?*; *It is doing something to the soil, what could it be doing?*; *Is the weather here similar to ours? How might it be different?*; *Do you think the rice plants growing would grow in our country?*

This kind of running commentary, from a birds–eye view (on the flying carpet) could be supported with pictures of different kinds of agriculture or farming from other countries. Different geographical and environmental factors that influence what and how foods are grown or farmed could then be introduced in an imaginative and creative way.

Extending learning

Mind movies can also be used to support children appreciating and understanding the food journey from the initial source to their dinner plate, by providing the children with a series of images or sounds of a market place or particular parts of the process, e.g. harvesting, the market, making noodles, the supermarket. Ask the children: *What (do they imagine) they can hear?*; *What (do they imagine) they might see?*; *Can they hear lots of people talking?*; *What are they doing?*; *Where do they think this might be?*; *What will it smell like?* Given a picture of people processing the food, e.g. making noodles: *What might they be making?*; *How will they eat their noodles?*; *Do you think they will just eat noodles?*

The mind-movies technique can be developed further. Once children have developed the skills of building up their own soundscapes (of a particular place or context) they can work in groups to develop these independently; groups of six work well. It is most effective if the children gain confidence in making soundscapes of more familiar contexts first. This will vary according to the life experiences of the children. It could be a farm or a busy market. Asking the children to work in groups of five or six, they can focus on a picture of, for example, a farm. The children can be encouraged to reflect on what they can see in the picture and consider the sounds that these animals or objects might make. They can then be asked to identify and practise the sounds. *Do they think it will be a loud or soft sound? Why?* Once they have identified their sound, the children can be asked to sit in a circle. The soundscape can then be (gradually) built up. The first child recites their sound continually, the second child then adds their sound. This continues until all the children in the group are contributing, and the cacophony (or not) of sounds completes the soundscape. The other groups can then listen to the soundscape and identify the sounds that they can hear and make suggestions about whether the animal or object is close or far away. They can do this by considering whether the sounds are loud or soft. Once practised, the different groups can be given different pictures and encouraged to develop varied soundscapes. The sound-scapes can then be performed, allowing the other groups to then listen to the composition and attempt to identify the noises (and work out what they represent) to make suggestions about where that soundscape might be, giving reasons for their ideas.

Development of skills and understanding

Mind movies proved to be a very effective technique for drawing on exist-ing ideas, whether they are from images in books, television or from the children's own life experiences. They can enable teachers to appreciate what their children are thinking from the responses to questions and tasks. This approach has effectively helped making growing plants more relevant as some children reported that they connected the plant growing with the food they eat. The approach also appeared to support children in understanding that food needs to be transported from one place to another and that this does not happen by 'magic carpets'.

Theme: Sport

As well as using the mind movie technique to take children to places that they cannot usually visit, mind movies can also be used to take children to places that can only be imagined. This can be great fun! Ask the children to work in groups of three. First the children think of a sport. Ask the children to think of a sport that they might want to play, or the children can choose a sport from a range of cards (see Table 5.1). Tell the children that they are at the Olympics and have been chosen to represent their nation for the given sport. The mind movies can then be used to transport them to this place and they can enact their sport. The children can then be 'transported' to an imaginary place where their equipment:

- becomes magnetic;
- becomes soft and sponge-like;

- becomes made of rock;

- becomes made of paper; or

- becomes made of plastic.

The children can be asked: *What can they see/hear/feel?*; *How do they know this place is like that?*; *What difference does it make to their sport?* This technique then links in very well with miming movement (Chapter 5).

Developing skills and understanding

Mind movies to imaginary places proved very successful, particularly when the children were invited to generate 'actions' that showed how they thought the changes in properties (e.g. becoming magnetic, being made of ice, etc.) of things (and objects) around them might impact on them moving (or living) in an everyday way. It immediately translated (for the teacher to see) the children's understanding of materials. The range of views that are shared in this way could become a starting point for an investigation. One child, for example, indicated that she did not believe that making a swimsuit out of sponge would make any difference to diving in a pool and swimming. This could then be used to discuss and contemplate, with a class investigating the properties of sponge and how the behaviour of the material might alter or change when placed in water.

Theme: Toys

In this theme, the initial stimulus for the mind movie could be a clock chiming. The children can be invited to imagine that they are in a toy shop and at the stroke of midnight they (as different toys) will come to life. They could be asked to consider: *Which toy could they be?*; *How might they move?*; *Does their toy spin, walk, roll?*; *Why is it hard to move like the toy? Why not?* The children could then become that toy using the technique of miming movement (see Chapter 5). This activity was most successful when children had the chance to explore (and play with) a range of toys beforehand. This meant that they could apply first-hand experience of touching the materials, examining the toys and what they were made of, as well as experimenting with the way the toys moved and reflecting about why they moved as they did. Alternatively, the activity could act as a lesson starter (and each child could be given a toy to mime) so that not knowing how the toy moved would provide a stimulus to want to find out (and be given a second opportunity to show how the toy worked). Another possibility is to take the children to worlds that are of different sizes. Older children could look at the ratios i.e. a world 1/10 of the size of today. *How would it feel? What difference might it make? What things could they still do? Couldn't they do?* see Figure 8.2. A further approach of using mind movies is for the children to develop their own ideas of a place by making up the soundscapes themselves. A stimulus could be a picture of a fairground. The children could work in groups looking at the picture, and be asked: *What can you see?*; *What sound might that make?* Children can then practise the sounds, e.g. clicks of the chains as a roller coaster moves, the cries of excitement as children go on the rides, the roaring sounds of generators, etc. They can then build up the soundscapes by repeating their sound and, as more and more children add their sound, the crescendo of a cacophony of connected and related sounds develops. Other groups can then listen carefully to try and identify the sounds. They can use this evidence to draw a conclusion as to where the soundscape might be, giving reasons for their choice.

Development of skills and understanding

Mind movies allowed the children to envisage very different worlds. It put them firmly in the shoes of the person/toy in that situation, allowing them to imagine what the experiences felt like first hand. It activated prior learning about materials, how toys were put together, how they moved and behaved. For example a spinning top – imagining that coming to life: *Why might you choose it/not choose it?*; *How does it behave?*; *Does it carry on spinning?*; *Is that all it does?*; *What happens if it is on different surfaces?* If a teddy was chosen: *How does it move?*; *Where are its joints?*; *How does that compare to us?*; *Are the things that it can do that we cannot?*; *What is different/the same about how we move?*; *Who would win in a competition to . . . spin? . . . run?* This provides many starting points for exploration.

Figure 8.2 Miming how different it would be travelling in a toy car ten times smaller than normal

Reflections from the classroom

One teacher said she thought that, 'Mind movies is a way of introducing the children to a topic. They use their imagination, are 'tuned-in' and then produce much more from their work' (year four teacher, North Staffordshire school).

Another teacher explained, 'I was always tempted to give the children lots of space around them to "widen" their vision of what they might see or imagine. Now I find it much better to keep people close together, especially if the class has children with a big range of abilities. Also in mind-movie exercises, where passing on the sound in a circle with eyes closed, very many children will open their eyes to have a look. Rather than seeing this as "cheating" or not doing it properly, it is usually a good opportunity to have some fun and enjoyable discussion about which animals we know that might have ears better adapted than ours to do this without looking' (year two teacher, North Staffordshire school).

In discussion about using the 'magic carpet' or 'helicopter' technique to imagine what we can see, teachers agreed that it is often important to think about how the children are seated or arranged. 'This is because some children will become engaged in the "imagining and seeing" more quickly than others. If some children are finding it difficult to envision what is being "seen" and spoken about, they may disengage and feel left out as others focus on a particular object or idea. If the group is gathered fairly close together and not spread out, it is easier for the teacher to encourage a group focus and spot children who need extra encouragement' (year five teacher, North Staffordshire school).

9

Mini historical plays and monologues

Introduction to the approach

Mini historical role play

This approach was developed to share with young children some relevant and interesting insights into a scientist's life and work. The teacher normally reads aloud an appropriate narrative of a scientist's life and work with the opportunity for the listening children to act out roles of different characters in the story or even to pretend to be the scientist and echo what they may be doing in their work. The PSTT website provides an example of this illustrated by a mini historical play (based on Mary Anning) that could easily be enacted by several groups of children. Stories about the work of any scientists (e.g., the Montgolfier brothers embarking on the first hot air balloon flight (see Figure 9.1) can be introduced through this technique.

Monologue

These are mini speeches, usually given as if from the scientist themselves. The monologues provide personal insights into the scientist's work and life. They could be presented by the teacher (dressed up with a few props), a teaching assistant or a child. There are also videos available (from the BBC 2014) that could be played for the children to watch. The monologues have been successfully used as an introduction to investigations that are similar or based upon work that the scientist may have done. William Harbutt's story, about the man who invented plasticine, could be used as an introduction to creating a modelling material (from a range of materials such as flour, water, food dye and salt).

Guidance to use mini historical plays (MHP)

This strategy can be adapted in a number of ways:

Figure 9.1 Children enacting the story of the French brothers who invented the hot air balloon

1. *Whole class participation*

   Reading a narrative that all the class can collectively enact, e.g. Table 9.1: Extract from the William Harbutt story. A philosophy for children approach (Lipman 2003) can then be applied to ask the children: *What do you know about this scientist?*; *What do you think you know?*; *What do you imagine?* Reflective discussion of these questions can draw out the characteristics of the scientist and his work and enable the children to empathise with him as a person. The children may suggest that they *know*, for example, that he is 'artistic', 'creative' or 'is thoughtful', 'has ideas'. They may also suggest that they think they know he is 'hard-working', 'determined', 'strict' or 'business-minded'. Suggestions about his image include 'tall', 'white-haired', 'a good father' and 'quite strong'.

   Appreciating and understanding the skills a scientist employs could also be consolidated by the children being invited to develop a 'character on the wall'. This is where a long roll of (plain wall) paper has a body out-line drawn on it and descriptive words are incrementally added to it (see Figure 9.2).

Discussing the range of characteristics that a scientist portrays (through engagement with the mini historical play (MHP) or monologue) better prepares the children to then sculpt a partner (see Figure 9.3) or build up a (small group) 'tableau' of his/her traits (see Figure 9.4).

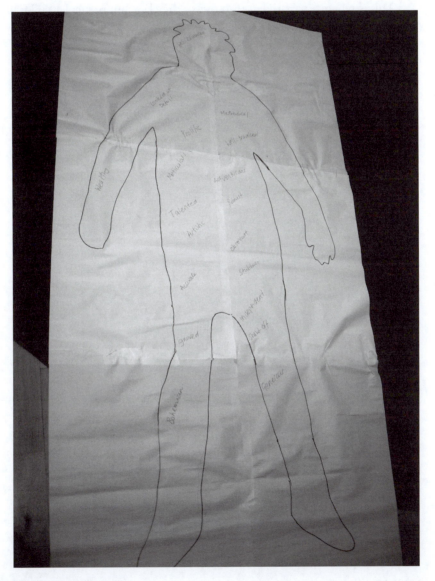

Figure 9.2 Character on the wall

To engage the whole class, the children can be asked to reflect upon the traits, skills and characteristics of the scientist. They might choose to depict the word 'puzzled', 'teaching' or 'hard-working', etc. They can then be invited in turn to walk into the centre of the class circle and bodily express their view of an aspect of the scientist's character. Each child adds to the whole class (3D picture) to gradually build the 'tableau' of the qualities of the scientist and the way he or she worked.

2. *Individuals within the class enacting specific roles*
    This is where a narrative is read out to the class, but particular children have specific roles, e.g. Table 9.2: Extract from the Josiah Wedgewood story. Children take on parts and enact what different characters might do as the story unfolds.

3. *Small group enactments*

    Having the children engage in a very simple mini role play, in a small group (see Figure 9.5a) with easy-to-follow scripts, e.g. The story of

Figure 9.3 Sculpting Harbutt

Figure 9.4 Forming a tableau of Harbutt's characteristics

Mary Anning (see http://www.azteachscience.co.uk/ext/cpd/dramatic-science/historical-play-monologue.html). Appendix 11 provides an example of a script that could be used to support this approach.

The story of Mary Anning could also be introduced through (a mind movie using) the nursery rhyme: 'She sells seas shells on the sea shore.'

This nursery rhyme could be chanted by the children with eyes closed, there could also be an audio recording of screeching seagulls and crashing waves against the sea shore playing to create a mind-movie introduction.

This nursery rhyme is reputed to have developed from the Mary Anning story (of a girl of thirteen and her dog) finding and selling fossils (and undoubtedly other interesting shells and objects) to visitors at the beach in Lyme Regis. Figure 9.5b illustrates how the children invited to depict Mary Anning's work have focussed on representing different fossils and one child is digging them up.

Figure 9.5a Three children enacting story of Mary Anning (the girl on the left is 'selling' her sea shells and fossils to the passers-by on the right)

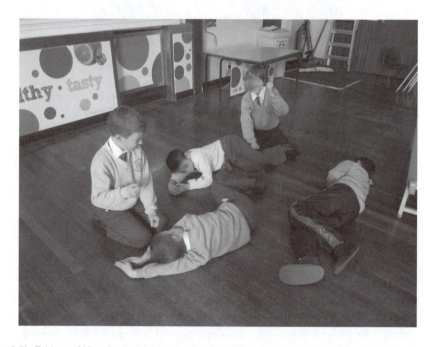

Figure 9.5b Tableau of Mary Anning's skills as a fossil hunter. Note some of the children being fossils

TABLE 9.1 Extract from the William Harbutt (the inventor of plasticine) story

Narrative as read by the teacher	Enactments by children in response to questions and suggestions in the narrative
This is the story of William Harbutt, born just over 150 years ago. He lived by the sea where there were lots of boats. He lived almost as far north as Scotland (Newcastle upon Tyne). Near where he lived there were lots of bridges made of wood, horses pulled carts, there were no cars, no computers, no televisions, no Xbox or DVD players. (*What do you think children did to amuse themselves? What would they play (with)?*)	*Playing with wooden toys, painting, modelling, etc.* *Enacting playing with spinning tops, big hoops, hop scotch, making models, painting, playing tig.* *Enacting painting on a big canvas.*
William was an artist. (*Can you show how he might do this?*) Then he became an art teacher. (*How would his actions change? Demonstrate what he might do when teaching art.*)	*Enacting teaching art (e.g. writing on a board, talking to the class, pointing to children).*
He had his students make models and sculptures with clay – but they found it hard to make small models of toy soldiers and small animals. (*Can you show how you might make a clay model?*)	*Enacting model making as a student in class.*
The headmaster (and others), though, thought it was too modern (they believed art was only about painting pictures!) for students to make model people or animals (like those on a farm). So William decided to start his own art school!	*Enacting how William would behave differently as a head teacher rather than just an art teacher.*
William cared about making the materials that his art students were using as well as he could, so that they produced excellent sculptures and models. He thought that the clay was heavy and difficult to mould (and as it dried out it became more difficult to change its shape), so he set about making a different material.	*Enact how modelling clay (and other materials such as jelly, glue paste, etc) would change if it dried rather than stayed flexible.*
Bill (an old soldier) helped him to mix big tubs of a softer paste (like putty) in the basement of the house. This meant that they had to carry salts and jelly to a large wooden tub in the cellar. They had to use their arms and hands to mix the putty-like material.	*In pairs, enact how Bill and William would struggle together to move the salt and jelly mixture down steps into the cellar into a big wooden tub and then mix it all together.*
When the mix was 'thick' they then pushed a heavy roller over it backwards and forwards to squash out the water (soaked up by rags at the side of the tub). The mixture was then left to dry for several weeks until it was just right for modelling.	*Continue in pairs as Bill and William, showing how they would squash out the water and mop up the water seeping out.*

TABLE 9.1 Continued

Narrative as read by the teacher	Enactments by children in response to the narrative
So William, with the help of the Bill, had 'invented' a putty-like material that could be handled and shaped and re-shaped many times.	*Enact being one of William's children, visiting the cellar, finding the modelling material and playing with it to make a model.*
He then thought it would be good to try it out with his children . . . he let them play with the grey, not too sticky, but soft squashy material.	*In pairs as two of William's children enact how you might add colour to the plastince and show how delighted you are that it is different colours for your modelling.*
William was surprised that his children liked making models with the special clay . . . and they came up with the name of plasticine! But he thought 'How could I make this grey-coloured putty more interesting?'	
His daughter Olive said she thought different colours would make it more interesting.	
With the different colours . . . the red, blue and yellow . . . the packs you could buy were called 'the complete modeller'.	
The plasticine become so popular that Olive (William's eldest child) and her father travelled around the world selling the modelling clay!	*Enact how Olive and her father might travel around the world showing and selling their wonderful invention.*

Using the story of Josiah Wedgwood

Preparation involves the teacher choosing children to be:

- Josiah Wedgwood (youngest of eleven children, age approx. nine years, disfigured and disabled with a weakened knee from smallpox);

- Thomas Wedgwood (older brother, in charge of the business since his father died);

- Mary Wedgwood (mother of eleven children); and

- the other nine siblings.

Mind movie introduction

This narrative could be introduced through a mind movie. Ask the children to close their eyes and imagine what these sounds (e.g. horses hooves on cobbled stones; pedalling noise to rotate the potter's wheel; the whirring sound of a

TABLE 9.2 Extract from the Josiah Wedgwood story

Narrative as read by the teacher (prompting the interpretative actions of the children in role if needed)	*Enactments by children in response to the narrative*
Imagine you lived nearly 300 years ago (no-one had been to the moon, people walked everywhere or travelled by boat or in a horse drawn carriage, there was no McDonald's or Pizza Hut, no cars or even tractors, no phones, computers or televisions) in Stoke-on-Trent (where most of the pottery came from at that time).	
You are going to visit your friends or family (like Josiah when he was five or six) that live the other side of the town, how will you get there?	*Walking or riding in a horse-drawn carriage to get across town.*
Your family had made plates, cups, teapots and sugar basins for years. All the family ever talked about over dinner was how to throw, turn, fire, paint and glaze pots and create crockery.	
Imagine you are sat around the dinner table, drinking and eating and telling your family about the process of making pot, cups, saucers, etc . . .	*In groups of eleven siblings and a mother enact how you might sit around the table for a meal and a drink . . . discussing making plates, pots and the family business.*
You are an able potter by the age of nine, you can 'throw' pots onto the wheel and shape them.	*Everyone sits as if (Josiah) at a potter's wheel and throws lump of clay on to rotating turntable and attempts to 'shape' it.*
You are good at it, so your older brother, Thomas, takes you under his wing as an apprentice. You observe carefully how to improve the quite coarse clay pots that are made. You experiment and realise how the clay can be refined and made smoother and more 'clean' in appearance.	
How can you show you are becoming 'better' at making the pots?	*The children enact potting quicker, making more, creating different shapes, etc . . . . stacking up around them.*
Your brother, though, does not agree to you becoming a 'partner' in the family business.	*Show how you would feel.*
Even though you are a skilled potter and have suggested quite a few ways to improve the pots produced, your eldest brother does not wish you to 'partner' him.	*Show how you feel now . . .*
You are upset by this and set up your own business, making pots your way. Your better glazing and decorating techniques are recognised by royalty and your company expands very rapidly.	
Your pots are highly prized and even royalty buy them (you have several kings and queens from around Europe visit and come to request special plates and pottery to be made).	*. . . and now . . . and what would you be doing?*

TABLE 9.2 Continued

Narrative as read by the teacher (prompting the interpretative actions of the children in role if needed)	Enactments by children in response to the narrative
What would dinner around the table be like now?	Enact fewer siblings and preparing for a queen/king to visit for dinner/afternoon tea.
As you get older, though, your weakened knee prevents you from continuing to work the potter's wheel pedal, so you focus more on other things, such as building a canal (the Trent and Mersey) with Erasmus Darwin to transport your pottery on barges up and down the country.	
You are good friends with Erasmus Darwin and he and you become grandparents to Charles Darwin (who proposed the theory of evolution!). You both chat about canals, rocks and all manner of things scientific.	Enact going to dinner, via horse-drawn carriage, to see other scientific and business friends. Discuss with a group of you what you might talk about at that time that would be important in science.

turntable; the chinking of bone china; the pouring of tea; stirring with a spoon in a teacup) indicate that life was like at the time this (young) scientist was growing up.

Props that could be used to help 'set the scene' and support the context of the narrative or story could be a rough clay pot and a smooth bone china (finely decorated) cup and saucer.

Development of scientific understanding and skills

Engaging the children in thinking about the life and work of scientists can help them to appreciate how they have certain skills in common with scientists. Selecting a scientist that they have heard of, e.g. Isaac Newton or Florence Nightingale, can aid their appreciation of 'what a scientist is' and 'what a scientist does'. They can also grasp how scientists have real families, siblings (e.g. Wedgwood who had ten siblings), pet dogs (e.g. Darwin who had beagles) and may also have poorly family members (e.g. Edison's deaf brother) or need to earn money to buy them food (e.g. Anning having to 'sell' seashells). Selecting a scientist that they may not have heard of, but who produced items that the children deal with on a daily basis, e.g. the inventor of Velcro (Mestral), plasticine (Harbutt) or making cups and saucers for royalty (Wedgwood) can inspire the children, grab their attention and even help them to believe that they could work scientifically, understand science and even become a scientist and make a difference to the world.

Developing the focus on (and of) different enquiry skills

The monologues and MHPs were devised to emphasise a range of enquiry skills.

TABLE 9.3 Outline of the key enquiry skills the MHPs and monologues (Appendix 1–20) were designed to highlight

Enquiry: Ideas and evidence	**Rachel Carson**'s detailed observations over time enabled her to identify the effect of insecticides on plants and animals (and habitats).
	Edward Jenner's observations led him to realise how smallpox could be prevented from spreading using cowpox 'pus'. His experiment on James Phipps provided evidence to show how immunisation worked.
	George Washington Carver made careful observations of the factors that could affect plant growth. He used the evidence to devise different ways to cultivate different crops.
	Ibn Al-Alhaytham watched how light behaved from his confined living quarters (using lenses and mirrors) and experimented to try to explain the way it travels in straight lines, can be reflected and refracted.
Enquiry: Planning an experiment	**Antoine Lavoisier** experimented and measured carefully how things changed when (burned in) air (and oxygen) and could combine with them to make new substances.
	Gregor Mendel experimented in the monastery with the peas grown in the garden. He showed how different features could be passed onto future generations.
	Alessandro Volta painstakingly planned how to layer copper, zinc and cloth soaked in brine to make the first battery.
Enquiry: Systematically testing ideas	**Antoine Lavoisier** repeatedly experimented and measured carefully how things changed when they were heated.
	Edward Jenner followed his predictions (that injecting James Phipps with cowpox would prevent smallpox developing) in a step-by-step way to check his hypothesis.
	Joseph Lister routinely applied disinfectants to evaluate the effect on operation and infection successes.
Enquiry: Exploration	**Humphrey Davy** was a chemist who discovered several new elements of the periodic table including calcium, potassium, sodium and boron. He also invented the Davy lamp for miners working underground.
	Luigi Galvani discovered the nature of electrical nerve impulses in animals.
Enquiry: Obtaining and presenting evidence	**Leonardo da Vinci** was meticulous in his observation and (artistic detailed) recording of his inventions and discoveries of the human body.

TABLE 9.3 Continued

	Florence Nightingale was systematic in the way she organised and presented data on illness as graphs, particularly pie charts. She used this kind of evidence to argue for hospital funding.
	Gregor Mendel investigated the genetics of peas and presented his findings as well-organised numerical evidence.
Enquiry: Considering evidence and making connections	**Edward Jenner** connected his observations about finding no smallpox disease in milk maids with the possibility of preventing the spread of the disease.
	Dmitri Mendeleev recognised how the mass, characteristics and behaviours of different substances fell into 'patterns' to form the periodic table.
	Joseph Lister reviewed the frequency of illness following operations carried out in different conditions and realised that carbolic acid was beneficial.
Enquiry: Solving practical problems	**Edward Jenner** immunised James Phipps with cowpox and then tested his idea by applying infected smallpox pus and waited to see if he survived.
	Leonardo da Vinci created various inventions such as the parachute, machine gun and armoured tank.
	Alessandro Volta invented an early portable form of electrical energy, the voltaic pile, which was the fore-runner of the battery.
	Joseph Shivers created a stretchy fabric (Lycra) that didn't lose its original form (and shape) even after being worn for a considerable length of time.
Enquiry: Considering evidence and evaluating	**Mary Anning** knew where to find good quality fossils. She could rapidly evaluate likely conditions for finding valuable relics in Lyme Regis.
	Florence Nightingale could synthesis the evidence and make informed decisions about where best to direct resources for caring for the wounded.
Enquiry: Communicating evidence to variety of audiences	**George Washington Carver** coded his secret recipes for making products from peanuts as well as writing general informative guidance for farmers cultivating crops.
	Leonardo da Vinci could convey artistic impressions of objects as well as provide detailed and annotated diagrams of scientific interest.
	Florence Nightingale summarised evidence clearly and precisely so politicians could understand the severity of a problem.

Example of a mini historical play: Joseph Shivers – the narrative that the teacher would read

This is the story of Joseph Shivers, born just over 90 years ago in America (the state of Pennsylvania).

Near where he lived was a wide river with sandy shores in a wildlife park, and when he was younger he was energetic and very keen on the outdoors, loved walking and was always looking around at nature and other people when on his walks. (*Can you show how he might have walked? And think about what he might have noticed?*)

When he was a student during the Second World War he helped to develop a medicine to stop soldiers becoming ill (from malaria) in certain hot countries (in the South Pacific, places like China and Japan). The malaria sickness made the soldiers sweat, get very hot, they had no energy to fight, they coughed a lot and their muscles ached. (*Can you show how they might have been on the battlefield if they had malaria?*)

It took Joseph two years to develop a medicine so that the soldiers would not get malaria from the mosquitoes in the countries where they were fighting. (*In pairs, can you show the difference between fighting if you had malaria and if you were fit?*)

Joseph's work on this medicine has since helped other scientists to develop lots of different medicines to fight malaria and prevent many millions of people dying.

Joseph was also interested in sport, particularly football, tennis and swimming. (*Can you show how you would move if you were playing one of those sports?*) He watched lots of matches (when he was about thirty – sixty years ago, in the 1950s). The clothes worn for these sports were long sleeved, covered your legs and were loose fitting – not at all elastic! They were made from material a bit like the sheets on your bed. Imagine you have only clothes made from cotton sheet-like material – *how would that change what you wore for swimming? Show how you would swim if you were covered in an all-over pyjama outfit, made of a cotton sheet (like swimsuits of the 1950s), that was not elastic at all!*

What happens to the swimsuit made of cloth? How does it affect your movements/ swimming? How easy was it to put the swimsuit on? How did you feel wearing the sheet-type material to swim in? How could sheets be changed to help you to wear them to swim in?

If it rained when you were playing football or tennis – how would your play be affected?

Joseph was asked by his bosses (at Du Pont) to secretly work on developing a more flexible material for famous women to wear as underwear – so that girdles made of bone could be more comfortable! Joseph carefully selected a team of scientists to work with him. *If you were Joseph – what kind of people would you want to work with you? Why?*

The scientists managed to develop a material that expanded and snugly covered the body contours, but after the wearer had been sat for a while and then stood up, the garment stayed crumpled. *What would that mean for swimmers, tennis players and footballers?*

For weeks and weeks the scientists repeatedly experimented with different combinations of various substances – but couldn't create one that was truly flexible, expanded, changed shape and then returned back to the original size and shape.

How do you think Joseph felt? What would you have done?

Joseph loved playing with chemicals, he liked to mix things together and see what happened. *Would that be safe for you to do?* He did all his experiments in a special room so that it was safe: in a laboratory. *What things do you think he used to mix chemicals and make different mixtures?*

Can you act out what he might have done?

Although other scientists had developed ways of making soft rather than rough materials to make clothes elastic, they stretched out but did not return to their original size and shape. Joseph played around with mixing different amounts of different compounds.

Eventually Joseph discovered how a substance that they had not tried could be added to make the material re-bound back to its original size. In 1958 he had created what we call today Lycra! A material that can stretch, remain supportive and comfortable, and then return back to its original form.

Who would find this useful? Why?

What clothing do you have that is like this?

Who at the Olympics, do you think, will be wearing Lycra?

So all of us here will, in some way, be using or wearing the fruits of Shiver's labours. All athletes, fashion houses and even medicine today owe a debt to Joseph Shivers, the inventor of an anti-malarial drug and Lycra!

Developing enquiry skills

Different aspects of different scientists' life and work can offer illustrations or opportunities for children to develop various enquiry skills.

The scientist can be introduced through the mind-movie approach (e.g. Mary Anning) that sets the time (or era when the scientist lived, as well as the location) for when the scientist was working. Once the children have explored the life of the scientist (through monologue or MHP) and reflected on how they worked (by forming a tableau or character on the wall) they can then emulate their skills when working scientifically themselves. The activities have resulted in children developing their own questions to be investigated too (Ofsted 2013).

Posing an investigative question or query that the children could work on an answer or response to might be, for example, the kinds of questions outlined in Table 9.4.

Exploring Shivers' work, for example, is illustrated in a series of photographs that comprise Figure 9.6, showing the way that Joseph Shivers' monologue

Figure 9.6 (a–l) A series of photographs to illustrate how to investigate from Shivers' monologue or MHP

(Appendix 13) can excite learners to devise useful investigations to explore the nature of different fabrics or materials (see Table 9.5). Following up the Shivers' monologue, appropriate enquiry questions could be:

1. What can you say about the material?

2. How could you find out which is the most effective material for an Olympian's clothing?

This experimental work was designed to consolidate: *Ideas and Evidence*; *Planning an experiment*; *Systematically testing ideas*; *Exploration*; *Obtaining and presenting evidence*; *Considering evidence and making connections*; *Solving practical problems*; *Considering evidence and evaluating*.

The equipment that can be provided to support the investigation includes:

■ various squares of materials such as cotton, jersey, card, bubble wrap, foam, foil, etc.

■ apparatus that means the materials can be investigated: washing-up bowl, jug, spoon, water, ruler, pegs, string, etc.

The photographs (in Figure 9.6) illustrate how the drama techniques of tableaux and mind movies were applied. There are also photographic exemplifications of the various 'steps' in the investigational process that was developed from the Joseph Shivers monologue (Appendix 13).

Developing enquiry skills from the Marianne North monologue are shown in Figure 9.7 a–e. The focused enquiry took the form of preparing for an expedition overseas and preparing paintings and drawings for an exhibition. Skills developed included: *Exploration*; *Obtaining and presenting evidence*; and *Considering evidence and making connections*.

Other scientists' work that was developed to support investigations were Newton and Harbutt's (see Figure 9.8 a–f).

The focused enquiries took the form of: i. What can you find out about each substance?; ii. Which is the best substance to model with? . . . and why? (Emulating aspects of Harbutt's work.) and: i. How many different ways can the toy move?; ii. Which (variable) makes a difference to how the toy moves? (Emulating Newton's work.) The experimental work was designed to consolidate: *Ideas and Evidence*; *Planning an experiment*; *Systematically testing ideas*; *Exploration*; *Obtaining and presenting evidence*; *Considering evidence and making connections*; *Solving practical problems*; *Considering evidence and evaluating*; and *Communicating about evidence*.

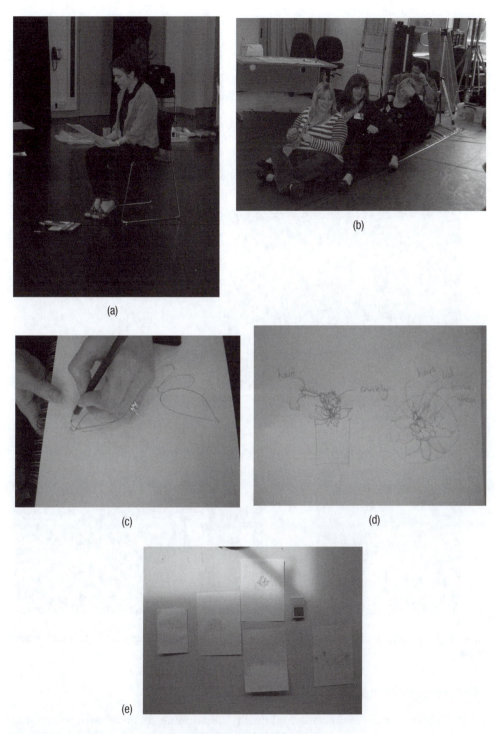

(a)

(b)

(c)

(d)

(e)

Figure 9.7 (a–e) Steps in developing enquiry skills like Marianne North

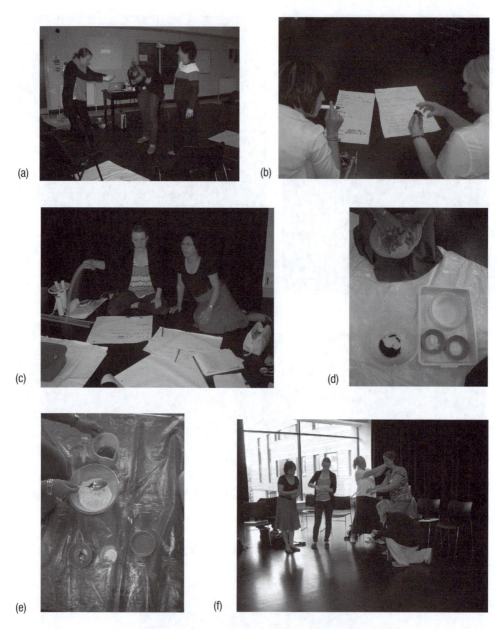

Figure 9.8 (a–f) Illustrations of the ways that being Isaac Newton or William Harbutt can help to develop enquiry skills

Effective questioning and good questions

To engage the children in good quality questioning the investigations need to be truly 'open', that is, they should have multiple responses or solutions that are

TABLE 9.4 Questions that could be posed to develop related experimental work

Scientist	Skills to emphasise	Materials	Question
Marianne North	Thinking creatively to explain things.	Quite coarse paper (black and white)	Which seeds are produced by which plant?
	Making comparisons and identifying simple patterns.	Charcoal, chalks	What do you notice about the fruit?
	Using observations and measurements to draw conclusions.	Water colours	Can you see any patterns?
		Pencils	Are there any fruits with similar structures?
		Different plants, fruits and seeds (the more exotic the better)	What can you tell me about the material?
Joseph Shivers	Testing ideas using observation and measurement.	Range of fabrics (e.g. jersey, cotton, wool), paper, card, bubble wrap	How could you find out which materials are effective for an Olympic sport?
	Trying things out (deciding about evidence, equipment and materials).	Bowl, bucket, jug, spoons, tape measure, ruler, water	What properties do you think it might need?
	Making a fair test.		How would you test it?
	Checking observations and measurements by repeating them when appropriate.		What materials might work well combined? Why?
	Making comparisons and identifying simple patterns.		
	Using observations and measurements to draw conclusions.		
Benjamin Franklin	Thinking creatively to explain things.	Balloons – different sizes, shapes and colours	What can you find out about static electricity?
	Asking questions.	Different fabrics, spoons, tissue, space blanket, foil, feathers, comb, rulers, paperclips, rocks, metals	What makes a difference?
	Testing ideas using observation and measurement.	Plant sprayers (to create different humidities)	How does static electricity affect our everyday lives?
	Trying things out (deciding about evidence, equipment and materials).		
	Making comparisons and identifying simple patterns.		
	Deciding whether conclusions made are supported by evidence.		

TABLE 9.4 Continued

Scientist	Skills to emphasise	Materials	Question
Michael Faraday	Testing ideas using observation and measurement. Trying things out (deciding about evidence, equipment and materials). Making a fair test. Checking observations and measurements by repeating them when appropriate. Making comparisons and identifying simple patterns. Using observations and measurements to draw conclusions.	Range of different batteries (3) Battery tester Additional wires Foil sheet Cork Rubber Shells Graphite pencils (9B, 6B, 3B, HB) Charcoal Wire wool Range of three rocks (inc haematite) Old fork Small squares of metal – nickel, cobalt, copper, iron	How many different ways can you make a circuit that works? What (variables) might make a difference to the circuit? What did you notice? Can you group the materials into those which allow the circuit to work and those that don't? Which materials allow the circuit to work? What scientific word could describe these materials?

TABLE 9.5 Suggestions about the way the use of MHP might progress in a lesson

Strategy	Description of strategy	Key learning objectives	Activities	Reflective questions to consolidate learning
Mini historical play (Josiah Wedgewood)	The teacher tells the group a story – which could be scripted. During the story members of the group become the characters in the story – they could be given a prop/costume item to signify who they are, or a simple line to say. There might be moments in the story when whole groups are engaged, or moments when they could offer their thoughts on the events of the story, e.g. a meeting. Through this enacting the story is brought to life.	To Identify personality traits of scientists from the past. To familiarise themselves with scientists of the past. To explore ideas on scientific thinking.	Children take on parts and enact them as story unfolds. Imagine you were six years old (child chosen to be six-year-old Josiah), suffered from small pox, your dad had died (father) but the older brother (of three brothers/two sisters) in the family offered you an apprenticeship in the family pottery business . . . Josiah watches carefully to see how the pots might be improved . . . What might you suggest to your older brother as the apprentice (learner potter) to improve it? Connection with the way we commemorate special events through special editions of crockery/mugs.	What did he do? Why do you think he . . .? What did he do that makes him remembered? How would he feel . . .?
Monologue (Joseph Shivers)	The teacher reads the monologue (or can listen to the podcast for Shivers).	To empathise with being Shivers. To consider how Shivers applied scientific skills (including thinking about: *Ideas and evidence; Planning an experiment; Systematically testing ideas; Exploration; Obtaining and*	The teacher can read out the monologue (or listen to the recorded podcast available on the PSTT website (p. xv) or through the BBC (2014) website). After listening to the monologue the following class discussion can be framed by these reflective questions: ■ What do you *know* about this person? (At least two facts you are sure of.)	Key questions: What do you know about this person? What do you think we know about the person? What do you imagine about them? To help with the tableau:

TABLE 9.5 Continued

Strategy	Description of strategy	Key learning objectives	Activities	Reflective questions to consolidate learning
		presenting evidence; Considering evidence and making connections; Solving practical problems; Considering evidence and evaluating) to develop Lycra.	■ What do you *think* we know about the person? (At least two things.) ■ What do you *imagine* about them? (At least two things.) The teacher can then be hot seated by the children (they can devise questions to ask the teacher-in-role) so that they can prepare to carry out experiments that relate to the work that Shivers is known for. A tried and tested approach is to organise the children into teams of three or four, provide samples of a range of different materials, e.g. sponge, bubble wrap, cotton, wool, spandex, paper or cardboard; and use these stimulus questions: ■ What can you tell me about the material? ■ How could you find out which material is most effective for an Olympic sport? Additional resources that they may need include: Force meters, rulers, weights, range of different materials, buckets, paper towels, string, scissors, Sellotape.	*What kinds of skills did this scientist show?* *How do you know?* (It would be helpful to collate responses on the board to remind the children when they mime his qualities.)

quite acceptable (and valid). These provide authentic enquiry learning opportunities for the children (as suggested in Table 9.3).

To empathise with, and rehearse, the kinds of skills that different scientists possessed, not only could the questions suggested in Table 9.4 be posed, but the children would propose ideas after the tableau or MHP activity.

Reflections from the classroom

One teacher reported that she had given the children lots of choice to explore the waterproof qualities of different materials. In the first session she asked them an open question, e.g. *Which material is most waterproof?* The children also asked lots of questions of the teacher, so they agreed a class question, the teacher provided them with limited equipment and lots of children chose different ways to do the experiment. When asked, 'Why are you doing it that way?' they would reply with a variety of reasons, indicating, 'Because of this and this and this'. The teacher noted that at first they found it difficult to really focus on one thing, but after more practice responding to open questions and devising their own experiments, the children became more confident and it was easy to just say, 'Right, now investigate what would happen . . .' and they could! (year four teacher, South Staffordshire school).

Another teacher reported how this approach helped SEN children in her class. She had already shared that the 'Years 5/6 love anything at all to do with drama so it's gone down really well in my class, but often they get carried away with the drama and perhaps lose an element of the science part of it. For example, when I gave them the static electricity investigation, the fact that they had no guidance from me, I said, "this is your investigation, this is what you've got, you go ahead", it totally and utterly threw them, so I've learnt that what I need to do is give them a few choices and limit it a bit more so that they've still got choice but they've got some guidance too'. She added, 'Once they were interested it worked and they showed their results' (year five/six teacher, West Midlands school).

10

Thematic approaches

Throughout this book there have been suggestions about the ways that drama can be used to develop children's understanding about science in various contexts: sports (or the Olympics), exploration (where new habitats, plants or animals may be encountered), desert island (where the main focus is 'survival'), food (to help children appreciate the need for a balanced diet as well as recognising where food comes from) and toys (where physical science, and topics such as forces and materials are important).

Figures 10.1 to 10.5 suggest different routes through these themes outlined in this chapter.

Schools, however, sometimes have cross-curricular themes that are predetermined, because all subject disciplines are planned to be aligned simultaneously. Table 10.1 has some suggestions about the ways in which the dramatic strategies have been organised to fit existing schemes of work in one of the project schools. These lists are provided as suggestions; they are not the definitive opportunities, nor an exhaustive schema, for dramatic science.

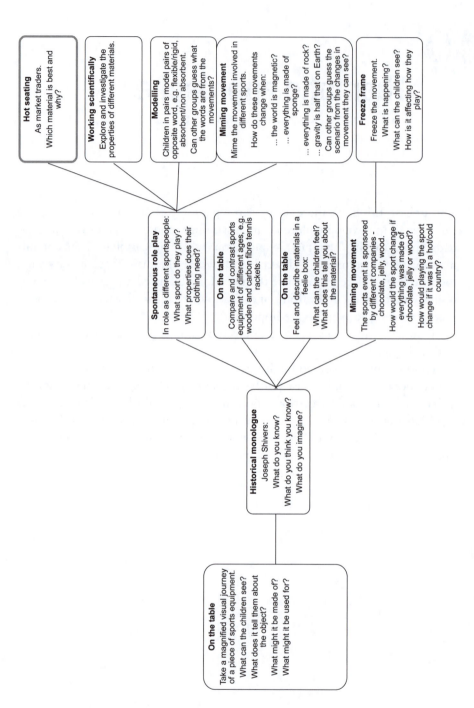

Figure 10.1 Drama route through sports theme

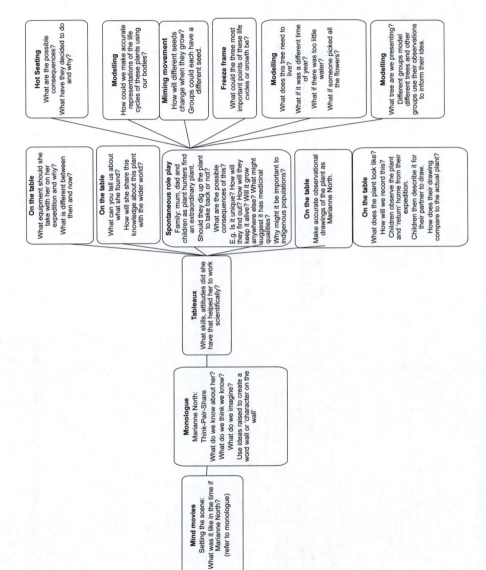

Figure 10.2 Drama route through an exploration theme

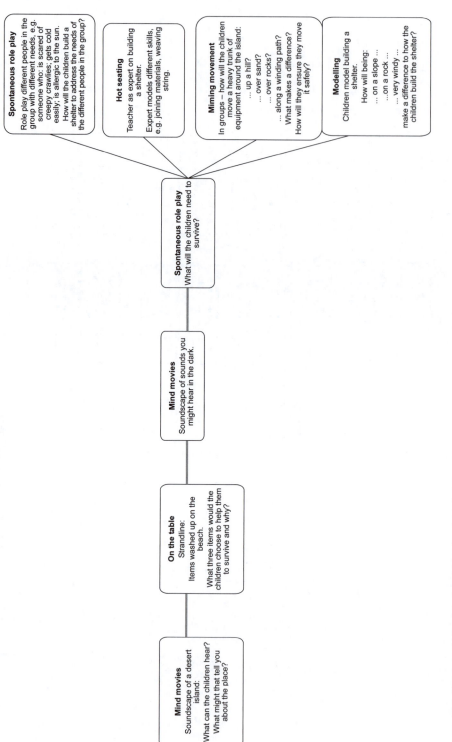

Figure 10.3 Drama route through desert island and survival themes

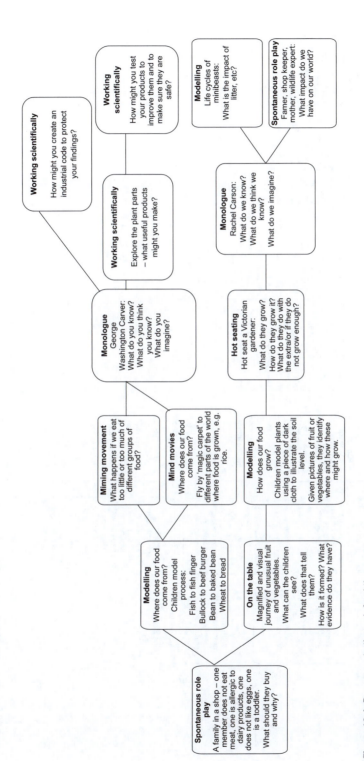

Figure 10.4 Drama route through food theme

The figure contains the following connected boxes:

Working scientifically
How might you create an industrial code to protect your findings?

Working scientifically
How might you test your products to improve them and to make sure they are safe?

Modelling
Life cycles of minibeasts:
What is the impact of litter, etc?

Working scientifically
Explore the plant parts – what useful products might you make?

Spontaneous role play
Famer, shop keeper, mother, wildlife expert:
What impact do we have on our world?

Monologue
George Washington Carver:
What do you know? What do you think you know? What do you imagine?

Monologue
Rachel Carson:
What do we know? What do we think we know? What do we imagine?

Miming movement
What happens if we eat too little or too much of different groups of food?

Mind movies
Where does our food come from?
Fly by 'magic carpet' to different parts of the world where food is grown, e.g. rice.

Hot seating
Hot seat a Victorian gardener:
What do they grow? How do they grow it? What do they do with the extra/or if they do not grow enough?

Modelling
Where does our food come from?
Children model process:
Fish to fish finger
Bullock to beef burger
Bean to baked bean
Wheat to bread

Modelling
How does our food grow?
Children model plants using a piece of dark cloth to illustrate the soil level.
Given pictures of fruit or vegetables, they identify where and how these might grow.

On the table
Magnified and visual journey of unusual fruit and vegetables.
What can the children see?
What does that tell them?
How is it formed? What evidence do they have?

Spontaneous role play
A family in a shop – one member does not eat meat, one is allergic to dairy products, one does not like eggs, one is a toddler.
What should they buy and why?

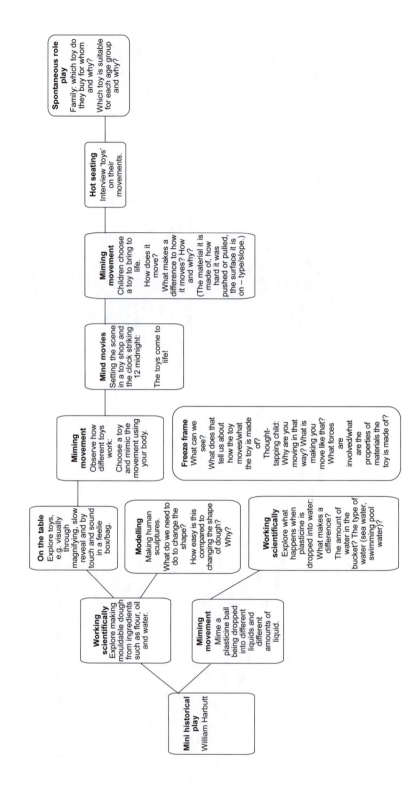

Figure 10.5 Drama route through toys theme

TABLE 10.1 A series of suggestions about the ways in which drama conventions could be incorporated in KS 1 and 2 topics

Plants and animals: KS 1	
Dramatic technique	*Activity*
On the table	■ Seeds ■ Different plants/fly trap ■ Nest ■ Fruits/vegetables
Hot seating	■ A seed underground – what is happening? ■ Habitats – why do you live here? ■ Features of animals – why do you have big ears, sharp claws, etc.?
Mini historical play	■ Steve Irwin ■ David Attenborough
Freeze frame	■ A seed growing into a plant – where is the fruit? ■ Life cycle of a tadpole/butterfly, etc.
Miming movement	■ A seed growing into a plant ■ Animal movements/minibeast movements ■ Where does food come from?
Spontaneous role play	■ Visiting the zoo ■ Working on a farm
Relevant books	■ The Enormous Turnip ■ Stone Soup ■ Jack and the Beanstalk ■ The Apple ■ From Seeds to Sunflowers

Materials: KS 1	
Dramatic technique	*Activity*
On the table	■ Different materials ■ In the box – hidden materials to describe properties
Hot seating	■ Market stall – selling different materials based on their properties
Mini historical play	■ Joseph Shivers
Freeze frame	■ Sports equipment made of different materials, e.g. a tennis racket made of jelly
Miming movement	■ Melting chocolate ■ Sports equipment made of different materials, e.g. a football made of ice ■ Swimming through custard, etc.
Relevant books	■ The Three Little Pigs

TABLE 10.1 Continued

Light and sound: KS 1

Dramatic technique	Activity
On the table	■ Unusual musical instruments ■ Different light sources ■ Coloured lenses/prisms
Hot seating	■ Playing different musical instruments ■ Market stalls – reflective materials
Mini historical Play	■ Louis Braille
Freeze frame	■ Playing different musical instruments – How is sound made? ■ Shadows – Where should shadow be?
Miming movement	■ How does a torch work? ■ Shadows ■ How to play different instruments
Spontaneous role play	■ Night time workers – What do you wear? How can you see?
Relevant books	■ Owl Babies ■ The Owl who was Afraid of the Dark ■ Peace at Last ■ Don't worry, Spike . . . about the Dark!

Health and growth: KS 1

Dramatic technique	Activity
On the table	■ X-rays ■ Food ■ Balloon heart pump ■ Items from different stages of growth – dummy, rattle, etc.
Hot seating	■ Child acts out roles of different ages – What do you eat?, etc. ■ Characters – Florence Nightingale, Mary Seacole, etc.
Mini historical play	■ Life of Florence Nightingale ■ Life of Mary Seacole

Dramatic technique	Activity
Freeze frame	■ Different stages – baby, toddler, adult, etc.
Miming movement	■ Keeping clean – brush teeth, wash hair, etc.
	■ Digestive system – What happens to food when we eat it?
Spontaneous role play	■ In the supermarket
	■ In a hospital
Relevant books	■ Titch
	■ I Will Not Ever Never Eat a Tomato
	■ Harry Goes to the Hospital
	■ Florence Nightingale (Famous Lives)
	■ Mary Seacole (Famous Lives)

Forces: KS 1

Dramatic technique	Activity
On the table	■ Different toys – How do they move?
	■ Toys from around the world
Hot seating	■ Different toys – How do you move?
Mini historical play	■ Nick Hornby
Freeze frame	■ Pushing/pulling boxes – post on Isle of Struay
	■ How do different toys move?
Miming movement	■ Pushing/pulling boxes – post on Isle of Struay
	■ How do different toys move?
	■ Wind/water driven objects
	■ Cars on a ramp – different surfaces
Relevant books	■ Pinocchio
	■ Someone Bigger

11 Assessment

Concern regarding science concepts

In science teaching, teachers are often very concerned with factual content they must cover. Their view of a successful lesson can be bound up with ensuring that the correct information has been effectively imparted. Using drama, however, can provide numerous opportunities for more imaginative ways for the children to learn through science, about science and to learn from science. They can engage with learning in a more active and participatory way. It can quite naturally (through modelling or miming movement, etc.) provide the arena for children to show what they think or believe about something. They often hold intuitive ideas, such as thinking that all plants are cultivated, therefore weeds are not plants (Guest 2003), or that a single wire connection from a bulb to a battery will make a successful circuit (because they see electrical appliances in their homes work with only one cable). Young children may also think that magnets stick to objects because they have magical properties or some kind of glue (Guest 2003). These kinds of alternate conceptions can be based on personal observations and their (limited) life experiences so far. Drama, therefore, offers an ideal opportunity to explore what instinctive ideas and prevailing perceptions exist and (often) persist in children's minds.

Children are their own agents of learning, which is particularly prominent in drama where their bodies (torso, head, mind and limbs) can all physically combine to communicate their ideas and thought processes. Reflection about how to act or perform can raise questions about science and how they themselves understand it. Drama itself, therefore, becomes a means of children realising what they know, what they are uncertain of and may even catalyse what they wish to find out more about.

As adults (and teachers) we often say things that can be misleading, such as, for example, that 'plant needs a drink' (but plants absorb water through their roots) or 'the jar is empty' (but there will be air in it that can't be seen with the naked eye) or 'the sun has just come up' (but in fact the earth has rotated).

These often 'throw-away' comments that we (and perhaps parents or other adults) utter can cause confusion for the children. So as teachers we need to know about the 'ideas that learners bring to their science education' (Harlen 2012: 44) so that we can more appropriately support them to form more accurate scientific ideas.

The dramatic science activities outlined earlier in this book have offered a wide range of approaches and ideas to help with this. In Table 11.1, there are some further suggestions (and activities) about ways that formative assessment may be utilised through drama.

Concern regarding scientific enquiry skills

There is 'a growing body of research evidence' (Harlen 2011: 7) that indicates scientific skills such as 'engaging in observation', 'considering [. . .] evidence', 'expressing [. . .] ideas', 'pursuing questions', 'using and developing skills of interpreting data, reasoning, proposing explanations' and 'reflecting self-critically' are not as well developed as they could be, because it is difficult for teachers to nurture these abilities in classrooms. Ofsted corroborate this by highlighting how there is a particular lack of development and understanding of inquiry skills (Ofsted 2011: 6) in primary education.

To address this apparent paucity of enquiry skills, teachers need to appreciate how to recognise and nurture them in science lessons. Drama, again through effective context setting (via the MHPs and monologues in Chapter 9) and immersion in purposeful and authentic tasks (e.g. Table 9.3), can help address this, but there also needs to be an appreciation of the ways that formative judgements of children's progress in these skills can be made. Later in this chapter there are suggestions about this. In Chapter 13 the ways that drama has impacted on developing these skills is discussed.

Why is assessment important?

Assessment lies at the heart of good teaching and learning (Harrison & Howard 2009). However, because judgements about children's learning can take place in many different ways, some are inevitably better for supporting successful learning than others. Since the removal of high stakes SATs testing in science, *some* teachers have readily developed creativity in their lessons (Ofsted 2011), while others have continued as if still preparing for the test!

The shift to teacher assessment at the end of KS 1 and 2 has offered more opportunities for learning in primary science to become more creative and less didactic. It is decreasingly concerned with *imparting* scientific knowledge, but more focused on exciting children about science and through science (Ofsted 2013).

Without any form of assessment teachers cannot make informed judgements about the progress that their learners are making. However, there are a wide variety of ways in which teachers (and pupils themselves) can make conversant assessments about progress in learning that are not just (narrow and limited) national summative tests!

The Assessment Reform Group (ARG) explain that research shows that improving learning through assessment depends on five key factors:

- the provision of effective feedback to pupils;

- the active involvement of pupils in their own learning;

- adjusting teaching to take account of the results of assessments;

- a recognition of the profound influence that assessment has on the motivation and self esteem of pupils; and

- the need for pupils to be able to assess themselves and understand how to improve.

(ARG 1999: 4–5)

Drama activities provide opportunities for children to discuss and share their ideas, reflect on what others offer as their interpretations of scientific concepts and then, in collaborative group situations, make justified decisions about *how to do something* or agree as a collective (small group or whole class) *what something is*. Through these kinds of processes they are continually engaging in informal peer-to-peer assessment as a natural part of the learning experience. Children actively enacting their ideas, viewing others' actional interpretations and then discussing how the actions illustrate (or not) the science can provide feedback to improve the *display* or artistic *conveyance* of a scientific concept. These processes, the children themselves recognise, support the development of understanding (Chapter 13).

The use of formative assessment to more effectively teach science with drama

Using drama to formatively assess what children think can provide rich feedback to teachers to help them reshape their pedagogy to better support more effective learning science. As Black et al. (2003) found when attempting to develop teachers' formative assessment practice, although science teachers could tell students what was right and what was not, they found it 'extremely difficult, if not impossible, to offer advice to the students as to how to improve' (ibid: 58). One of the reasons for this was that the tasks were not rich enough to provide informative evidence for the teacher to make judgements and proffer suggestions to the learners about how to further develop their knowledge, understanding or skills. McGregor and Precious (2010) and McGregor (2012a) have found that drama offers many ways to provide 'rich' authentic learning tasks that can be utilised to 'see' what children think. Teachers reflecting more carefully about what they observe from children's enactments of their thoughts can support more focused professional development discussion about how the 'next steps' in teaching which can in turn further support and enhance learners' scientific understanding. In other words, using the drama performances to inform judgements about progress in learning can help teachers to better hone feed-back and feed-forward (Harrison & Howard 2011).

As Brodie (2010) clearly indicates, assessment for learning should lie at the heart of effective teaching. His discussion highlights how it helps teachers to recognise learners' strengths and areas that require further development. Using drama to teach science emphasises this, as expressed by teachers who say, 'We have a 9–10-year-old child who is a bright sort of child who, when asked what she knew about planets she said "well I know that the moon is made of cheese" . . . it was quite an eye opener . . . these perceptions have just gone on and because they've [the children] not bought them up you've just never had to . . . you know . . . tell them that the moon isn't made of cheese!' (McGregor 2012b). Expression like this from the teachers illustrate how, not only do more of the children's ideas need to be uncovered by the talking and acting through the drama, but also there needs to be professional discussion about the ways in which the drama can then be used to effectively develop or reshape those alternate conceptions.

Ofsted, the inspectorial office that monitors the quality of learning in England, corroborates this by highlighting primary teachers' lack of understanding of enquiry skills and the provision of appropriate professional development (Ofsted 2011: 6). Concerns in primary science, therefore, are not just centred on conceptual development, but also include appreciation and application of science process skills, that is 'Scientific Enquiry'. Ofsted 2013, though, indicates that staff are now becoming more confident in supporting children to enquire. To continue to support scientific enquiry or work scientifically, theatrical approaches that merge the cognitive and affective domains (Duit & Treagust 2003) have been designed to support learners to redevelop and further hone their limited or naïve understandings, and are shared in this book.

Alternate understandings

There are many articles written, and studies conducted, that explore understandings that children hold. In this chapter, the focus is only on one area of the curriculum (chosen as an example) to highlight how knowing what children struggle to comprehend can inform what we should focus on as teachers.

Alternate understandings or partial understandings (often referred to as mis-conceptions) that children hold about 'food', includes understanding that:

- there are good and bad foods;

- energy and strength result from exercise not nutrition;

- food and drink travel separately through the body;

- stones can grow (anything in the ground grows);

- trees, plants and seeds are not alive (because they don't appear to move on their own);

- the bigger the plant the healthier it is;

- seeds come from a packet (not from an adult plant) and seeds have a baby plant inside;

- plants will grow without light as long as they have water;

- death is a reversible process!;

- cows lay eggs (two per cent of eight year olds believe this);

- eleven per cent of eight year olds did not know that pork chops came from pigs;

- eighteen per cent of eight year olds did not know where yoghurt came from;

- eight per cent of eight year olds from urban homes did not know that beef burgers came from cows; and

- eleven per cent of eight year olds did not know cheese was made of milk from a cow.

(Source: Manchester Evening News 2007)

There is developing research evidence (McGregor 2011, 2012) that suggests that children can understand more difficult ideas through engaging with drama to learn science. Therefore science activities that are purposely designed to help children to engage more fully in science to try to address alternate understandings (or further develop, as yet, immature understandings) can help children to better appreciate demanding science concepts.

Using drama to assess what children think

The following photographs were taken when children were asked to show what they thought happened when seeds germinated:

These photographs (Figures 11.1–11.2) show how the children perceive that the germination of the seed is above the soil (the brown cloth). Figure 11.3, though, shows how the children perceived that the seeds germinated and grew from below the soil surface (green cloth).

This group recognised how the location of seeds in relation to the soil was important.

Figure 11.1 A group of year four children depicting how seeds germinate. The brown material represents the soil

Figure 11.2 A group of year four children showing what happens after seeds have germinated

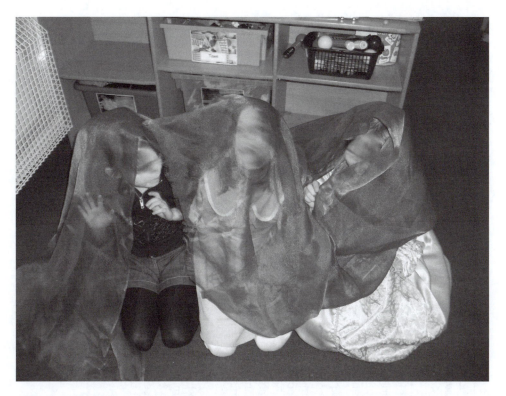

Figure 11.3 Three children in the process of showing how seeds germinate under the soil surface

In both cases, arguably, the children could be applying a correct interpretation. They are often shown how (or sow and germinate themselves) cress seeds that sprout on top of filter paper. However, when sowing seeds in a garden, frequently the seeds need to be dug into the ground to germinate (so that they are not eaten by birds or they remain moist, etc.) for the seed coat to be broken and the shoot and root to develop. What is important in learning science (and in this case, through drama) is that the children are invited to explain why they have demonstrated their ideas in the way they have, so that the teacher can (informally) assess their level of understanding. Even better is the opportunity for the remainder of the class (who may also hold different interpretations of the importance of soil, water, light, etc. in germination) to engage in a reflective discussion that draws on their personal experiences of seeds emerging from dormancy to develop into plants (and the factors that can influence the process). For the children to discuss and consider how different understandings of germination can hold true in particular situations (e.g. cress seeds or carrot seeds) is an approach that should be encouraged in science classrooms.

TABLE 11.1 To suggest where assessment opportunities might arise through the use of drama when teaching the 'food' topic

Theatrical strategy	Application to support learning within 'food' topic	Example(s) of application to assess prior understanding before teaching 'food' topic	How the strategy could support self assessment	How the strategy could support peer assessment	How the strategy could support teacher assessment
Mind movies	i. Can be used to 'transport' the learning to a different time or place, an approach to 'set the scene' for subsequent activities, such as: *You are on a farm, in the middle of a field . . .* *You are a (sycamore, acorn, dandelion, etc.) seed . . .* *You are a bee . . .* *You are a sheep . . . . . . how would you . . . ?* ii. Immersion in a topic to develop and employ a richer vocabulary.	Asking children: 'What would it be like to be a . . .? Where would you live? Why?'; 'What it is like . . . where a . . . grows?'; or 'Where do we get . . . (foods) from? How do we get . . (foods)?' disclosures their understanding of environments and what might live there and why, and how things are grown and processed (to make the food we eat). This is also a good technique for assessing children's use of scientific vocabulary (different parts of plant, process of pollination, growth, etc.).	Stimulate critical appraisal (discussion) of what others currently know and understand. In suggesting what the sounds (or other clues) might mean (for the context of the science) the children may be very creative in their thinking and convey it through their discussion with others (e.g. they realise that eggs are produced from hens, cheese is produced from milk that cows make and wheat grown in fields (from seeds) is used to make bread, etc.).	Children could experience mind movies and then in small groups, through shared conversations, agree what the mind movie portrays, recognising the contributions that each have made to the group perspective.	Children explaining what different locations might be like for different plants or animals (organisms) to grow in. Children clearly able to connect natural growth processes and manufacturing steps that result in producing the food we eat.

On the table	The whole class or small groups are presented with different seeds (e.g. pepper, cucumber, poppy, apple, etc.) or unusual plants (e.g. starfruit, gourd, etc.) that are magnified, viewed from different perspectives, etc., and they are invited to conject what the seeds might grow into and why, and what might be eaten of different plants parts.	Close observation of an unusual plant or seed and discussion about what it might be, what it might grow into and which part might be eaten (and why) can help teachers to uncover aspects of children's understandings.	Reflecting on observations of different plant parts or seeds to reason and justify what they may grow into.	Small group work (face, shoulder or diagonal partners) and intergroup exchange supports peer assessment. Shared discussions that build on each other's suggestions and ideas about what things could be (and why).	Ability to develop ideas from evidence, knowledge and understanding used in reasoning, e.g. smooth or rough surface of a seed, pip or nut, due to the way light is reflected from it. The children can be asked about other things that they are reminded of that are similar in some way.
Miming movement	Acting out ideas about how different seeds develop and germinate (e.g. sycamore, coconut, cress). Also different ways that plants grow and which parts of it become food (e.g. carrots, apples, grapes). Applies gestures and bodily actions.	How actions indicate whether a plant grows above ground, below ground, etc. What happens first or next; sequencing of events.	Elicits what the children's understandings are. Can provide pre- and post-teaching assessment of learning how things grow or how different foods are made.	Using the carousel approach, each group or individual takes a turn to show their ideas and then the other children give positive comments and perhaps a suggestion about how it could be different.	Giving individuals or small groups different foods to show how they have been produced can illuminate how they conceive of the derivation of things that they regularly eat, but are not straightforward to produce, e.g. muffins, pizza, cheese, yoghurts, sausages, etc.

TABLE 11.1 Continued

Theatrical strategy	Application to support learning within 'food' topic	Example(s) of application to assess prior understanding before teaching 'food' topic	How the strategy could support self assessment	How the strategy could support peer assessment	How the strategy could support teacher assessment
Freeze frame	Freezing action (as miming movement) above to create a still moment-in-time image. Usually managed by a tap on the shoulder or clap of hands.	Stopping at key moments in time as an acorn develops from dormancy to a full grown oak tree, for example.	Individually enacting and recognising 'key moments' in growing and food processing.	Having watched one group's *mimed* and *frozen* actions, another group has to provide the commentary for the enactments.	Children's commentaries of each other's actions (showing growth of trees or particular plants) provide rich assessment opportunities for the teacher (the actional interpretation and the verbalised interpretation of ideas conveyed).
Modelling	This is a static representation of an organism or object, whereas miming movement is concerned with how an object/organism works.	What is a vegetable or a fruit? How are they different? Where on a plant is the edible part? How is the edible part made?	Elicits what the children believe or understand. Can provide pre- and post-teaching assessment of learning. Can highlight what is understood about how and where food comes from (and the differences understood between plants and animal sources).	Groups or individuals are asked to model where (and how) the fruit and/or vegetables we eat grow (on a their respective plants), e.g. strawberry, tomato, potato, apple, raspberry, broccol).	Observers are asked to direct how the actors should change their model to show the difference in development of a strawberry plant to a raspberry cane, for example.

Hot seating	The group or class ask questions of the character or expert-in-role.	Asking questions about an experience after exploring or doing something, e.g. visiting a farm or the Victorian gardener.	Constructing (higher order) questions (for a purpose). Critical reflection of being in the hot seat.	Of the questions asked, peers could then be asked how they might be improved/ changed for a different purpose or a different character in the hot seat (e.g. when is best time to harvest the fruits or vegetables for a farmer or a rabbit or a bird).	Observations of the changes in questions for a different purpose or to a different character in the hot seat.
Spontaneous role play	Participants take on a role, such as the gardener or maybe a garden pest (slug, aphid, etc.) and improvise how they might behave towards each other in summer.	Given the scenario of a toddler, mother, grandmother who has trouble with her teeth, father who does not like meat and a child who is allergic to peanuts doing a weekly supermarket shop.	Contribute to discussion and argumentation of the science issues around buying different food for a family or preparing a celebratory meal for friends with varied dietary concerns.	Children could peer assess different groups' suggestions about the ideal shopping list; the menu for a meal, etc.	Draws out understanding of what children comprehend about the spontaneous role play scenario, e.g. understanding of what to choose to meet everyone's needs and give a balanced diet.
Mini historical plays	Teacher tells the group a story, which could be scripted, during which the members of the	In small groups, show the different between milk straight from the cow, milk that is sterilised and milk that is pasteurised.	Individual comments illustrating awareness and visualisation of a scientist's life and work.	Different groups devise questions to interview a scientist, with others deciding	Have the children act out how milk changes (and the effects) if it is left out of the fridge for a minute, one hour,

TABLE 11.1 Continued

Theatrical strategy	Application to support learning within 'food' topic	Example(s) of application to assess prior understanding before teaching 'food' topic	How the strategy could support self assessment	How the strategy could support peer assessment	How the strategy could support teacher assessment
	group are asked to become characters in the story (e.g. Louis Pasteur's discovery of pasteurisation).			what they may say as the scientist, e.g. Louis Pasteur being interviewed for the local paper after discovering pasteurisation! Or interviewing Washington Carver because he has produced more than 101 uses of a peanut!	two days, and request a (representative) commentary from Louis Pasteur about what is happening.
Monologues (and subsequent emulatory investigations)	A speech from a well-known scientist providing insights into their life and work.	Washington Carver and his discoveries about the 101 different ways that peanuts could be used.	Appreciation of a scientist's skills through using ideas and evidence, planning an experiment, systematically testing ideas, obtaining and presenting evidence, considering and making connections, solving practical problems, considering evidence and evaluating, communicating evidence to a variety of audiences.	Peer assess each other's experimental design as well as the 'products' produced at the end.	Teacher assessment of whether children can make connections to how science is used in real life, e.g. some might use the plant to make dyes, smoothies, cosmetics (e.g. facial scrubs). Teacher assessment of skills of working scientifically as children will need to test their products.

Table 11.1 summarises the different ways that the drama techniques could offer assessment opportunities, within the context of food.

Assessment opportunities

Formative assessment can be utilised at almost any moment of a drama activity. Through attempting to 'translate' or 'enact' how to be something or 'show' what might happen or has changed, the children are reifying their ideas through their conversations, actions and bodily configurations. They can even become reflexive agents of their own active learning when they see (in a mirrored room or through photographs or videos of themselves) how they have shown less force to kick a melting football, or sunk slowly into the water as the jelly canoe gradually dissolves in the river. Through watching each other they can also peer assess (and be guided by the teacher to apply Assessment for Learning, or AfL techniques, e.g. two stars and a wish, etc.) to reflect on the ways that the drama effectively conveyed good ideas and also how it could be further improved. Some of these opportunities have already been outlined earlier in the book. Table 11.1, though, attempts to summarise how a framework could be constructed to highlight in a scheme of work how assessment opportunities could be promoted through theatrical techniques. The theme chosen to illustrate the principles is 'food', but it is possible to apply the approaches to 'forces', 'sports', 'exploration', 'light', 'sound', etc.

Teachers' reflections

The ways that drama can help SEN children has been agreed on widely by the teachers. The development team agreed that children with special needs dislike writing and are turned off science because of that, but drama is a way of often 'assessing and taking them through an investigation where they use other skills' (year six teacher, West Midlands school).

Another teacher explained, 'I've really only got one SEN child this year and I've used these techniques to assess the sound and hearing topic and I am much more confident in my assessment of his learning through that topic because he could show me in this way rather than have to rely on something written or drawn . . . he basically refuses to write and his drawing wouldn't really show me much at all so for assessment purposes I am much more confident' (year five/six teacher, North Staffordshire school).

'The drama techniques are an effective way to assess learning [. . .] my class were confused about pollen . . . they didn't appreciate that pollen was male and needed to be transported to the female part of the flower so it was very good at revealing that' (year six teacher, Mid Staffordshire school).

Another teacher described how she, 'had children miming what they thought happened to bowls of different temperature of water over time, the misconception that though it cooled/heated up, really hot water would end up still hotter than ambient temp. This was addressed by further teaching/ practical learning, then the drama again showed how they had now understood and consolidated this knowledge' (year four/five teacher, North Staffordshire school).

12

Conceptual understandings developed through the dramatic approaches

This chapter is added to the book to help to provide a summary or overview (which will be more understandable if you have read through all the earlier sections) of the ways in which the drama can scaffold and mediate learning in science.

The activities offer a supportive framework, from which teachers can then question, explore and extend the way that the children reflect and think about the scientific concepts and processes introduced through the materials.

Table 12.1 below attempts to capture the range of scientific understanding that could be nurtured through the theme of toys (as an additional example to previous themes presented in the book).

TABLE 12.1 A summary of the ways in which the drama conventions can support development of different scientific skills

Theatrical strategy	Application to support science learning	Example(s) of application in the project	How the strategy supports understanding of science concepts and the development of scientific skills
Mind movies	Can be used to 'transport' the learning to a different time or place, an approach to 'set the scene' for subsequent activities.	Horse hooves clipping the pavements, distant ships horns, tinkling bicycle bells can recreate typical street sounds during the time of William Harbutt (the inventor of plasticine).	Asking good questions. Thinking creatively. Reflecting critically. Applying rich vocabulary.

TABLE 12.1 Continued

Theatrical strategy	Application to support science learning	Example(s) of application in the project	How the strategy supports understanding of science concepts and the development of scientific skills
On the table	The whole class or a small group are presented with an object (often unfamiliar). The object may be scrutinised from interesting angles with magnifier or slowly revealed. This can also be developed through a feelie box approach, where children can not see the object, only touch it. Class peers can ask questions that can be answered only through *yes* or *no* responses.	Close observation of an unusual toy. Elicits preconceptions about the objects/ things being scrutinised.	Encourages observation skills. Develops reasoning. Fosters recognising and describing characteristics of objects and organisms. Elicits preconceptions about the objects/ things presented. Supports development of formal science register from informal language.
Miming movement	Acting out ideas about how living/inanimate objects work. Applies gestures and bodily actions.	Showing how a ball (of different materials) behaves when dropped onto the floor or into a (half-filled/full) bucket of water.	Elicits the nature of children's existing understandings. Can provide pre- and post-teaching assessment of learning.
Freeze frame	Freezing action (as miming movement) to create a still moment-in-time image. Usually managed by a tap on the shoulder or clap of hands.	Stopping at key moments in time as a spinning top, jack-in-the-box or a clockwork character.	Articulating and describing happenings. Explaining scientific ideas. Critical reflection.
Modelling	This is intended to be a representation of an organism, object or process. Sounds and words can be used.	Enacting how different forces move objects, how a spinning top works, or a jack-in-the-box or a clockwork character.	Elicits what the children believe or understand. Can provide pre- and post-teaching assessment of learning.

Hot seating	The group or class ask questions of a character or toy-in-role.	As parent, what kind of toys are best for different children and why.	Constructing (higher order) questions (for a purpose). Critical reflection.
Spontaneous role play	Participants take on a role and improvise within a given scenario.	Market-place activity: buying (toys) presents for different family members. What for whom and why?	Discussion and argumentation of the science issues.
Mini historical plays	Teacher tells the group a story, which could be scripted, during which the members of the group are asked to become characters in the story.	Harbutt's creation of plasticine involving his family and an old soldier friend.	Develop awareness and visualisation of a scientist's life and work.
Monologues (and connected follow-up investigations)	A speech from a well-known scientist providing insights into their life and work.	Harbutt's reflections on his development of a special clay that became a world-wide phenomena.	Appreciation of the way in which these people worked scientifically to develop their ideas and communicate them to the wider world.

The thematic approaches outlined in Chapter 10 are suggestions about how the themes presented in this book can be approached in a variety of ways. The skills that the children develop can be influenced through the sequence (or order) in which the drama activities are encountered and, also, by the way that the teachers invite the children (as individuals, carefully organised groups or randomly selected partners, etc.) to engage with the strategies.

Working scientifically

Teaching to help children to work truly scientifically is a real challenge in primary classrooms. Drama can help with this as it can immerse the children in being a scientist.

In Chapter 9, the ways that stories or narratives about different scientists could help to scaffold and mediate children's inquiry skill development (see Table 9.4) were introduced. This section of Chapter 12 takes the ideas a little further to consider how these then can frame related (investigative) tasks that provide a rich contextual, and directly applicable, way to immerse children in being scientists.

Context setting

(A soundscape and/or a mind movie introduces when the mystery scientist lived and what they did.)

↓

Listen to the monologue

(This can be read by the teacher or a child, a pre-recording played or even a video of an actor-in-role as a scientist, e.g. Mary Anning, available at http://www.pstt.org.uk/ext/cpd/dramatic-science/resources.html.)

↓

Reflective elicitation of understanding(s)

(From the soundscape and/or mind movie and monologue discuss and share what is known, thought or imagined about the mystery scientist, so far.
The name of the scientist can be revealed at this point, but it may have little meaning if the children are not already familiar with that particular person.)

↓

Co-constructing appreciation of the scientist's traits to reach an achievement

(Through reflective discussion about information that has emerged about the scientist from the monologue, the children, in groups, can form negotiated and agreed representations of the scientist's character in the form of a tableau, e.g. Lavoisier's characteristics depicted in Figure 6.1.)

↓

Working scientifically to collaboratively develop understanding(s) about science processes through investigating

(Through engaging in an authentic investigational activity that can directly emerge from reflections about the scientist and what they did, the children can engage in developing their understanding about how scientists and science works.)

Processes for the teacher to mediate during this step:

- clarifying children's perceptions about how they might tackle the investigational task;
- sharing possible varied perspectives and approaches;
- providing range of suitable materials for children to choose from;
- helping children decide how to focus on what matters;
- co-constructing workable, plausible solutions; and
- decision-making in small groups to agree the best way to address the task.

↕

Reflecting on what happened (how investigations were carried out); what findings emerged and what it means about science and working scientifically

(After practically carrying out the experiments, the children share how they did it and what they found out. This could be by straightforwardly 'explaining' to the rest of the class and demonstrating how they used their equipment or in other more sophisticated ways, using technology and photographs, etc.)

Important reflection for the teacher to support:

- Disseminating/communicating the outcomes of the investigation (both *how it was done* as well as *what was found out* and if time . . . *how did it feel working like that scientist?*)

Figure 12.1 Outline framework for using drama to support more authentic investigations

The way that established drama conventions might be used in sequence is suggested in Figure 12.1. This offers a clear framework that has been shown to help teachers to improve the ways that their children develop inquiry skills (see Chapter 11).

To fully appreciate the kinds of questions that are appropriate to follow on from the monologues to engage the children in authentic investigations, Table 12.2 suggests what may be helpful for the children to consider.

This overview provides suggestions about the nature of investigational activities that could be used to demonstrate an aspect of the way in which the particular scientist worked. The monologues provide the introduction to the context of the scientist's life and work. A further discussion through thinking about what is learned from the mini speech, what has been inferred and what is imagined can contribute to the way that the children begin to consider and appreciate scientific ways of working through focusing on a particular scientist.

TABLE 12.2 Outline of the key enquiry questions or follow-on activities, linked to scientist's work, to scaffold more purposeful and authentic investigations

Investigational skill	Scientist displaying the skill	Follow-up investigational questions or activities to help the children	Suggested materials to be available for the children to select from
Enquiry: Ideas and evidence	**Ibn Al-Alhaytham** watched how light behaved from his confined living quarters (using lenses and mirrors) to explain the way light travels in straight lines, can be reflected and refracted.	■ Explore what happens when light is shone on different surfaces. ■ Which arrangement of torch, mirrors and lenses shows that light travels in straight lines?	Darkened room Various lenses (concave, convex, rectangular) Various mirrors (straight, curved, geometric shapes) Torches
Enquiry: Planning an experiment	**Rachel Carson**'s passion to preserve the environment informed her detailed grasp of the habits and habitats of animals in North East America.	■ Which kinds of rubbish, do you think, can be harmful to living creatures? ■ How might you test the effects of different kinds of rubbish on living creatures (without harming them)?	Seeds, kitchen towel, fruit shoots, coke, washing up liquid, crisp packets
	Antoine Lavoisier repeatedly experimented with combustion of different elements to produce his theory of conservation of mass (that even if substances changed their form, the total mass remained the same).	■ Explore what happens when the different coloured ice cubes are added to cold and warm water. ■ Consider when you created a purple-coloured solution and an orange coloured solution. Write down the steps for some-one else to be able to do it.	Jug of cold water (coloured blue with food dye) and a jug of warm water (coloured with red dye) Ice cubes made from water (coloured yellow) Ice cubes made from brine (coloured green)
Enquiry: Systematically testing ideas	**William Harbutt** used his experience of painting and sculpting with different materials to experiment with different clays, oils and other substances to create various colours of (modelling clay) plasticine.	■ How can you combine the different substances to make a modeling dough? ■ How can you test if it is effective? ■ Which is best to model with and why?	Flour Oil water Salt Jug Plastic floor covering

Enquiry: Exploration	**Benjamin Franklin** connected his observations about the ways that different materials behaved when the weather (e.g. thunderstorms) changed.	■ What can you find out about static electricity? ■ How does static electricity affect our everyday lives?	Balloons – different sizes, shapes and colours Different fabrics, spoons, tissue, space blanket, foil, feathers, comb, rulers, paperclips, rocks, metals Plant sprayers (to create different humidities)
Enquiry: Obtaining and presenting evidence	**Michael Faraday** experimented meticulously and presented his findings to the Royal Society in London through practical demonstrations of his ideas.	■ How many different ways can you make a circuit that works? ■ What (variables) might make a difference to the circuit?	Christmas tree bulbs Wires from a Christmas tree bulb circuit Variety of batteries (varied voltages) Spoons, tissue, space blanket, foil, feathers, comb, rulers, paperclips, rocks, metals
Enquiry: Considering evidence and making connections	**Joseph Shivers** created a stretchy fabric that didn't lose its original form (and shape) even after being worn for a considerable length of time.	■ What can you find out about the materials? ■ How could you find out which material is effective for an Olympic sport/ athlete?	Variety of materials (foil, card, bubble wrap, jersey, elastic) Jug and bowls Water Spoon String Paper towels
	Mary Anning knew where to find good quality fossils. She could rapidly evaluate likely conditions for finding valuable relics in Lyme Regis.	How could you explain the following series of fossilised footprints, made millions of years ago, uncovered, in turn when the rock faces were exposed.	Cards or enlarged illustrations of three imprints found at successive times illustrated

TABLE 12.2 Continued

Investigational skill	Scientist displaying the skill	Follow-up investigational questions or activities to help the children	Suggested materials to be available for the children to select from

Fossilised imprints found first:

Fossilised imprints found next:

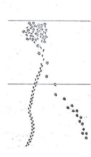

Fossilised imprints found last:

Source: (Collins 2011)

Plant materials could be: berries, nuts (beware of peanuts), red cabbage, red onions, large/numerous flowers of same kind Pestle and mortar
Chopping board
Plastic knife
Filter paper
Muslin
Bowls
Jug Hot and cold water
Spoons

Enquiry: Considering evidence and evaluating

George Washington Carver coded his secret recipes for making products from peanuts as well as writing general informative guidance for farmers cultivating crops.

Choose a plant or part of a plant

- In your group decide how you could investigate its uses.

- Keep notes – but think about how you can make sure others do not steal your ideas.

- You need to note what you did and how it showed the use of that plant.

- If you have time, try out the same tests again with a different part of a plant (are your notes good enough to ensure your group could repeat these tests exactly?).

Enquiry: Communicating evidence to a variety of audiences

Leonardo da Vinci was meticulous in his observation and (artistic detailed) recording of his inventions and discoveries of the human body. He communicated to others in a variety of ways (paintings, drawings, technical annotations, etc.).

In pairs (in separate rooms):

- Create a timepiece or clock using the materials available.

- Measure as accurately as possible one minute.

String, weights, containers, peas, beads, lentils, pasta, funnel, tubing, jug, water, etc.
Stiff parchment paper
Feathers
Ink
Charcoal

TABLE 12.2 Continued

Investigational skill	Scientist displaying the skill	Follow-up investigational questions or activities to help the children	Suggested materials to be available for the children to select from
		■ Use the digital timer to check the accuracy of your timepiece.	
		■ You will be required to write instructions for others to replicate it . . . so keep notes if you think that will help.	
		■ Draw a diagram of your timepiece.	
		■ Add notes and/or instructions so that another group can build a copy to check and see of it works.	
		Whole class reflective discussion: Whose is closest to timing exactly one minute?	
		■ How could you change it to measure five minutes or an hour?	
		■ How did it feel having to note what you did, using limited resources?	

13

Evaluation

This project has been run with over forty teachers, for different phases (KS 1 and 2) during the last three years. The following summaries of evaluative feedback are indicative of both the teachers and children who have participated in trying and testing out the drama ideas in schools in the Midlands.

The teachers' learning story

This reporting approach is adapted from Carr (2001). Through various means (discussions at workshops, annotating reflective journals, etc.) the teachers shared their learning stories. There appeared to be obvious stages in development that the teachers progressed through. Although some teachers had used drama approaches previously, prior to trialling the activities described in this book, most had only applied the techniques to teach literature or English. None of the teachers involved had utilised the full range of strategies developed and described in this book.

The stages of development that the teachers appeared to progress through are:

Act 1: Developing and establishing understanding

When first engaged with using drama to teach science, the teachers indicated that it took a while to become competent and confident in using the drama strategies. At first the 'on the table' approach had the biggest impact, with children often enraptured looking at objects they had never seen before, and even those that were familiar, but observed from an unusual viewpoint, were intriguing and activated curiosity. Initially the most challenging approach was the spontaneous role play and the MHP. However, as time progressed the teachers maintained that the 'Monologue was great . . . provided the wow factor as an introduction', and suggested that 'Monologues are good to introduce a topic, they get you to think differently about the scientist'.

Act 2: Persisting in creating opportunities

Many of the teachers had not used the strategies to teach science, and the children did not always find it easy to enact their ideas or to think about questions in hot seating, for example, but persisting in practising the approaches meant that 'the more experience they get at doing them [the techniques] the more likely they are to have a good discussion but not the first few times' remained true. It was important that the teachers themselves saw the value in the drama, so that they recognised the benefit in the effort needed to organise and manage the room, furniture and other curricular demands to include the dramatic approach. The view was that there was a long-term gain of using drama was sustained because, as a teacher previously stated: 'Pedagogically, approaches can be used to open things out, to check prior understanding, to check understanding after teaching and as an immersive experience over a whole day. Long term impact on learning was evident at the end of a unit.'

Act 3: Becoming more confident and creative to overcome challenges

Initially there was often a lack of confidence in the teachers applying such a different approach (even though experienced teachers were on hand to proffer advice), and although the investigational aspects seemed at first challenging, even for KS1, the teachers reflectively discussed how to differentiate and found that it worked with their children back in school.

Act 4: Realising drama can consolidate learning and enhance retention

As confidence and expertise grew, teachers recognised 'pupils retained their learning when questioned in later weeks' and one experienced teacher regaled narratives of children remembering the drama to learn about plants, electricity and other aspects of science . . . even years later!

Act 5: Drama enlightens teaching and learning

The teachers themselves realised that they were learning, not only about science, but also the enquiry skills of designing simple experiments and making measurements with simple equipment. They also reflected on how they were working in similar ways to real scientists and that they were developing the skills (see section on quantitative measure of impact) that they perceived were difficult to learn and teach.

Act 6: The finale: Embedding it into practice

At the end of the project, on the final workshop day, the teachers recognised how far they had developed their confidence and expertise in using drama and understanding science. They were all planning how they would ensure it

Enquiry: Planning an experiment

i. asking questions;

ii. considering sources of information;

iii. trying things out (deciding about evidence, equipment and materials); and

iv. designing enquiries (observing over time, pattern seeking, identifying, classifying and grouping, comparative and fair testing, and researching using secondary sources).

Enquiry: Obtaining and presenting evidence

i. using simple equipment and materials and controlling risks;

ii. making systematic observations and measurements; and

iii. checking observations and measurements by repeating them when appropriate.

Enquiry: Considering evidence and evaluating

. making comparisons and identifying simple patterns;

. using observations and measurements to draw conclusions;

. deciding whether conclusions made are supported by evidence; and

. using scientific knowledge to explain evidence, data or conclusions.

Most of the teachers indicated that some of these enquiry skills were better taught and enjoyed by the children after employing the drama strategies.

The findings indicate that there is variation in the extent to which the drama aids understanding of complex ideas, but nonetheless it enhances children's appreciation and understanding of scientific processes.

The participant teachers were also asked how they thought the drama had helped their Special Educational Needs (SEN), English as an Additional Language (EAL) and Gifted and Talented (G & T) children. The highlights in Table 13.1 illustrate the varied views that teachers held

continued to be integral to their teaching in years to
scheme of work that one school developed is provided

The teachers also noted how they changed their p
increasing their use of:

- magnification of dramatic/unusual objects to stim
- magnification of objects to stimulate children's sci
- magnification of objects to stimulate children aski
- drama and acting out ideas in science to uncover
- miming movement (of science concepts/ideas) to
  thought;
- hot seating (taking on specific views to support de
  skills);
- freeze frame (stop and explain a mime);
- role play (children taking on specific roles);
- mind movies (playing out in head possibilities in di
- stories about the lives and work of scientists; and
- stories about the lives of scientists to develop inv
  scientific thinking.

  All the above developments in teaching appeare
  changes in practice.

The teacher's reflective comments also indicated hov
agogy (not only, simply through using more of the
children understand science concepts better, but al
to hone their investigational skills (McGregor 2012
gational skills are difficult for primary teachers to
manner (so that the children become active, part
own learning). The approaches, though, that the a
that the children could work together practically
ence investigations that, to some extent, resonated
scientists might undertake. The investigational skil
ities (particularly the monologues and follow-t
augment include:

Enquiry: Ideas and evidence

i. thinking creatively to explain things; and

ii. testing ideas using observation and measurement.

TABLE 13.1 Collation of teacher statements about how they felt drama helped their SEN, EAL and G & T children learn science

How does drama helped SEN children:

- Super with SEN children.
- To involve themselves without feeling pressured because all children feel out of their comfort zone.
- How to explain what has happened during an investigation instead of formal recording. Understanding concepts.
- Joined in more – worked in teams. Didn't have to write results. Oral work too.
- Explore ideas without being put off by more able children. Demonstrable knowledge without paper (writing!).
- More inclusive in general.
- Allowed them to show their learning easily; broken down barriers.
- The children can explain their ideas and news easier through the drama rather than 'formal' recording.
- Given them greater confidence.

How does drama helped EAL children:

- Some challenge in this aspect.
- Okay but with tableau – children find it difficult to explain.
- Understanding concepts – actions shown as well as carrying out the action themselves.
- Understanding concepts and explaining.
- Good discussion with each other.

How does drama helped G & T children:

- Super with G & T children – used in science club.
- Children have thought creatively to think of different ways to present ideas.
- One child found it difficult to show his investigation as he wanted to write it down.
- Led groups. Had challenges – raised more questions. Some weren't so sure of themselves as they like questions that they can answer.
- Made more challenging 'science' accessible to them; developed vocabulary and questioning skills.
- Very engaged and can be further challenged by the science.
- Given them strategies to have an 'emotional' response to scientists and science concepts.

Response of SEN and EAL children

One teacher commented, 'I think the SEN children enjoy it (year 5) because it's practical, it's engaging and they are working in a very active way rather than sitting, but I did struggle with the EAL children with the language difficulty because I think they don't understand the subtlety of the questions, so translating them and trying to explain to them it doesn't seem to go quite the same way, so you need another adult to explain this is the concept we are doing' (year four teacher, West Midlands school).

Even though some EAL children struggled a little to grasp some of the concepts involved in the drama activities, it was generally agreed that in the longer term they would improve their understanding. As one experienced teacher suggested, 'Just watching from the outside, they are going to pick up more by seeing actions and reactions than [from] a printed page with words they cannot read' (year six teacher, West Midlands school).

Interestingly though, another teacher (year three teacher, Mid Staffordshire school) said this: 'I did dramatic science with mine and the SEN children actually and children who are sort of average found it brilliant. We did an experiment and they had to actually model it to me and show me what they did and they did it in groups so the other children had you guess what and how their experiment worked out. One of my boys is EAL, he is not gifted and talented but he's very, very clever, could not cope with it at all because he has to write everything down. It has to be on paper. He couldn't stand it to the point that he was in tears because he didn't want to do it. He didn't want to model or show it or even explain it, he just wanted to write on paper. But also talking to my bilingual assistant she says a lot of EAL children at home, their parents like them to write stories and that's why our reading is down because the parents don't hear them read as much because they think writing is much better and shows that they are really clever. But it was a really good session for me and the other children found it fascinating.'

Another teacher (year three teacher, Mid Staffordshire school) added that 'The children in the class that struggle with their writing, they were the ones that were coming forward and they were also showing us things like – we did some miming linked to the Olympics and some of our SEN children – some of the things they did out of school which we didn't even realise, they were just loving it. The language that was coming out because they were explaining everything they were doing was fantastic and they surprised us how confident they were and they are not usually like that.'

Another teacher thought that drama was something of an equaliser: 'Alongside the more traditional approach it sort of equalises the class more. It stops the ones that always dominate who are confident in their traditional approach taking over. It's probably more a case of integrating than replacing' (year four teacher, Mid Staffordshire school).

The children's views

All the teachers involved in trying out the dramatic science activities were asked to survey their children to find out what they thought about learning through drama. Tables 13.2 and 13.3 summarise the views of those that replied.

When the children were also asked about the ways that using drama to learn science helped them with their enquiry skills, the following table indicates the ways in which enquiry was supported.

TABLE 13.2 Summary of the responses from the 5–11-year-olds involved in the project

	% of children that agree with the statement	
	5–7-year-olds	8–11-year-olds
Using drama to learn science . . . is more fun	85	80
Using drama to learn science . . . helps because we act things out more	74	72
Using drama to learn science . . . helps me to understand harder ideas	69	55
Using drama to learn science . . . helps me learn more	58	62
Using drama to learn science . . . helps because we talk about things more	59	60
Listening to stories about scientists' lives helps me to understand how scientists work things out	Task too complex for the 5–7 year olds	61

TABLE 13.3 Children's reflective responses to a questionnaire about which aspects of scientific literacy and inquiry drama helped them understand

Aspects of scientific enquiry (and literacy) supported through dramatising science learning	Percentage of children that replied drama 'helps' with particular enquiry skills
asking questions	84
thinking of new ideas	88
testing ideas	83
explaining things	83
using simple equipment	71
being safe	77
making observations	81
making measurements	62

TABLE 13.3 Continued

Aspects of scientific enquiry (and literacy) supported through dramatising science learning	Percentage of children that replied drama 'helps' with particular enquiry skills
sorting things	81
seeing patterns	75
using evidence to make conclusions	78
knowing how to improve experiments	74
using scientific words	78

The findings indicate that the drama appears to mediate and help children connect their everyday lives with science so that the activities are meaningful (Neelands 2002: 4) and engaging (Varelas et al. 2010).

It would appear that the children are agentive in their own learning, they can engage their (minds and) bodies on multiple mediated levels (Varelas et al. 2010: 302). When using drama to learn science, there is a combinational application of mind and body, augmenting learning on several planes. First, the way as material objects they [the children] moved through space, then as social beings negotiating with each other how to interact and finally as metaphorical entities determining how to enact a representation. Augmenting this with historical narratives and speeches from scientists not only brings the science alive, but also provides authentic settings with rich opportunities for children to directly relate to the science concepts and processes so they can better comprehend scientific ways of thinking.

The drama techniques, devised specifically for science teachers to address the concerns outlined in the introduction, have shown themselves to be very appropriate to scaffold and mediate more effective learning. Not only do the drama techniques illuminate how young children are thinking, they also offer salience for all kinds of learners.

Previously Varelas (2010) conceptualised drama approaches that support improvised performances in science (such as miming movement, freeze frame, modelling, etc.) most appropriate for the younger children. Neelands (2002) has described how drama generally can mediate learning, but not specifically science. Yoon (2006) has begun to categorise scripted and non-scripted drama techniques to teach science, but has not embraced such a wide range of techniques as identified and evidenced in this book.

The activities and approaches described in this book attempt to conceptualise the nature of theatrical strategies that can mediate particular sorts of scientific skills and understandings, which extend beyond current evidence in the literature.

CHAPTER

14

Conclusion

The insightful application of drama to teach science

The various drama conventions outlined in this book, and the particular activities described for each convention, as well as the monologues (Appendices 1–20) can extend and enhance teachers' pedagogic repertoire quite significantly.

The evidence indicates that the theatrical strategies can help teachers to:

■ improve their understanding of living process, materials and their properties, physical processes;

■ enable better understanding of writing scientifically and the associated skills (asking questions, thinking of new ideas, testing ideas, using simple equipment, explaining things, making measurements, sorting things, seeing patterns, using evidence to make conclusions, using scientific words and solving problems);

■ ensure science learning is more appealing, relevant, participatory and pleasurable;

■ develop a more inclusive (rather than elitist) experience of learning science; and

■ empower children to become active agents of their learning.

The activities engage the children in an absorbing way, so that they become immersed in learning about and from science. It appears that the monologues and follow-up activities can help them personally relate to the scientists' lives and the ways that they worked to solve problems and make discoveries.

The task-rich learning opportunities (Wiliam 2011) such as those provided throughout the book also offer exemplary contexts for formative assessment (Black & Wiliam 1998).

There is still more to do, to further hone and develop how to use drama effectively in the teaching and learning of science, but if we, as the teachers and children involved in the project have so far, continue to pursue these avenues of exciting science lessons, then there may be many generations to come that will say of their learning in science, it is good because:

'I think drama makes science interesting because it is fun'
'you can run around and have fun, its active not just sitting down writing'
'you act out and you can see what it is and helps me'
'you hat to yous your amagenashon'.

(year four children, North Staffordshire school)

1a

Mind movie: Introducing when the mystery scientist lived

Antoine Lavoisier

Drifting in and out of a dream, the sudden feeling of a hot sun burning on to your eyelids and the clammy wet grass beneath you, brings you out of sleep. Opening your eyes slowly, you squint into the light and for a moment your mind is blank. Then, as always happens, you remember how you came to be here, lying under the trees. Last night, when the thunder storm came, you thought you would shelter from the hammering rain, here in the woods. Looking down at your feet, you see that the rain water has washed them; last night before the storm they had been bleeding and filthy, your shoes had fallen apart miles before you got here, their soft cloth no help on the rough stony roads.

Then, an old familiar feeling grips you, that sharp bitter pain of hunger. When was the last time you ate? It must have been the bread given to you by the people who let you ride on their cart, was it yesterday or the day before? But what does that matter? When you get to the city there will be plenty to eat, you have heard the travellers talking about it. In Paris, there is enough for everyone! The King and Queen have gone and now the people, the ordinary people, can share everything out between them. And you begin to imagine what sort of feast will be in store; meat roasted on a hot spit, the rich smoky flavour fills your mind and your mouth begins to water, baked apples, sweet and juicy, pastries dusted with sugar, just like the ones you always looked at in the baker's shop at home, except this time, you will be able to taste one yourself. It must be true, you've heard them talk of it and if you ignore the pain from your feet and the pain from your stomach, it won't be long before you're there. Last night, when you asked, the people pointed in this direction; Paris can't be far now!

So, you start, and as you go, the empty spaces of the countryside begin to fill with bustling carts and shouts of children, and the lanes have become streets, filled with busy rushing feet. Now, something else fills the air . . . can it be? Yes, chestnuts roasting over a fire, and next to them, loaves of bread, fat and fresh as can be. You reach out to take a small round loaf and feel a stinging blow to your head and a shove – an enormous hand is throwing you away from the stall. How can this be, in Paris, there is bread for everyone!

You limp away; now that you have stopped, the pain in your feet has returned.

Now, as you look up, you see a crowd, just a stone's throw away. There's shouting and whistling and you see a wooden platform. It's just like the carnival back at home. You make yourself very small and weave your way to the front; at least there should be something for your eyes to feast on. On the platform, there's a man in a white shirt, a handkerchief around his neck, and around his black hat there are ribbons of red, white and blue. He is dipping a broom into a bucket of water and sweeping it into the crowd, the pink droplets fly into the crowd and there's more cheering.

All of a sudden, you are lifted towards the sky and rough hands gather you up. 'You'll see better up 'ere, young 'un' says a man's voice as he plonks you on to his giant shoulder. A woman next to him pushes something greasy into your hand – chicken leg! No thought, just bite and swallow. As you close your mouth around the precious meat, a man is pulled on to the platform, he has a loose white shirt and his hands are tied behind his back. Your mouth gapes and, still with the food in it, you ask, 'Who is that?' 'A traitor' comes the quick reply; 'calls himself a scientist, if you please!' There are cackles of glee around you. 'He'll get what's coming to him, like the rest of 'em!' comes a new voice. Then, all the heads turn, a giant wooden frame, the 'traitor', 'the scientist' is pushed towards it and lies on his front. The sun is still hot and there is a glint, a flash, as you suddenly see a blade. A rope is pulled and you shut your eyes, tight. Perhaps, you never really woke up this morning, after all.

1b

Monologue: Our minds not our heads

Antoine Lavoisier

Paris 1794, 51-year-old Antoine Lavoisier sits with his hands tied behind his back (do not disclose the scientist, just the year and place, if you think that will increase the intrigue).

The air in here is foul. Foul, foul, foul! Still, what does it matter? I will not have to suffer it for much longer. Soon, I shall be out in the fresh air for a last look at my beloved city before my head is cut off. And when the guillotine comes down and my head drops into the basket, I expect the executioner will brush my blood into the crowd as he washes the scaffold down. That always makes the crowds cheer. At first, the people were hungry just for bread and now they are hungry for revenge. They wish to punish everyone they believe made them suffer, the King and Queen, the aristocrats. It is true, I have been a collector of taxes, but I only ever worked to help my country, I tried to improve the prisons and hospitals and I never tried to surround myself with riches. I was happier surrounded by the instruments in my laboratory. But at my trial the judge did not listen, he did not care about my work, my experiments. He said, 'The revolution has no need of scientists'.

Now, it seems strange to me that a person like myself who has devoted himself to the study of the air around us should now be about to lose his own breath forever. I was fortunate that my dear wife Anne-Marie was able to read English and translated the work of the great scientist Joseph Priestley for me. Mr Priestley made discoveries to greatly admire, his work in separating the gases of the air, magnificent! However, I did not think that all of his ideas were quite so true and, believe me, it was no easy thing to stand against the ideas of such a great man as Priestley.

My wife was also my greatest help in the laboratory – the work I did needed the most precise instruments and the results recorded most carefully. So when

I performed my experiments on combustion Anne-Marie was never far away. I burned mercury in a jar so no air could get in and no air could escape. I measured that about one fifth of the air had not been used up, and that the air which remained would not support life or burning. I carefully removed the red material that appeared and heated that in the same way. To my amazement the amount of gas produced was exactly the same as had disappeared! The gas produced allowed small animals to live and allowed the flame to burn brilliantly. When I mixed the two gases it behaved in the same way as air. The combustion itself does not take away the air, but turns it into something else: Standing air (what we now know as carbon dioxide). Of course, there were setbacks, but I never ignored results that did not always agree with my ideas; I returned to the laboratory and thought about it all again.

Many thought I had been brave to stand against the ideas of the most respected of scientists, but now a different sort of courage is needed as I hear them coming for me. I gave my life to oxygen; now there is very little left for me.

2

Monologue: Predicting from patterns

Dimitri Mendeleev

1892, an elderly man is in his study at the University of St. Petersburg, shuffling through a stack of papers and letters.

Dear Sir, we greatly admire your work . . . Dear Sir, we would be honoured if you would come to speak to us about your work . . . Dear Sir, your contribution to science is beyond compare . . . they are trying to flatter me. What do you English say? They try to 'butter me up'. I suppose I should not complain, for a man whose family came so close to disaster, I have much to be grateful for. Disaster is the only word I can use for something that in just one night changed our lives forever. That night, it wasn't just the sight of my family's glass factory burning to the ground; it was the sight of my mother, watching in horror as she saw everything that she had worked for destroyed. Strange that in so much heat people can actually look frozen. My father had already died and now once again we had to make sense of something so cruel and impossible to understand.

My parents had thirteen children and so my mother was left with little time to think or understand. She had to start again for all our sakes and she made sure that I still got my education. Now that education has led me to try and make sense of the world, to find meaning in nature. And it is the very elements of nature that have always fascinated me; I'm talking about the substances such as oxygen, hydrogen and calcium that cannot be broken down further into anything simpler. I wanted to understand what it was that these elements, so different in nature, could have in common, how they could be grouped together. I wrote books to help my own students understand. But, I knew that a system to truly understand how to group and categorise these elements remained a mystery.

Then one day, almost like a game, I wrote the name of each element and everything that was known about them on a card. I then began the shuffling and the re-arranging until, exhausted, sleep overtook me. When I awoke, I saw that the cards had slipped from my grasp and were now across the floor. Stiff and sore, I reached to pick them up and as I began to collect them, a thought dawned on me that had not occurred before. It was by weight, that is, the atomic weight, the mass of each element that we should order them. It became clear to me as I began this ordering that there were such differences in weights between the lighter and heavier elements that there must be others that we were still missing, and for these we must leave gaps in our system.

It was like having a huge table and the whole family has been invited for dinner, but so far only certain people have arrived. If we see children sitting down, we assume there will be parents, so we leave space for them and we can assume there will also be grandparents, so spaces should be saved for them, too, it's logical. It was the same in my system; the whole chemical family had not yet arrived, so gaps were needed to welcome them. After seeing so many senseless things, I had found something that made perfect sense and, just as in a real game of cards, logic and luck had played a part.

But now I must answer these letters after all, like the elements themselves, we all have our part to play.

3a

Mind movie: Introducing when the mystery scientist lived

Edward Jenner

Listen, what can you hear? Can you hear the steady tick, tick, tick, tick of the grandfather clock in the hall? Soon it will strike and echo all around the quiet house. A door clicks opens, footsteps, who can it be? There is a faint swishing and the sound of heavy chairs being moved and scraped across the floor. It must be the maid sweeping the floor in the study. There isn't much to do except sweep the floor, she is not allowed to touch anything else, not the books with their leathery covers, not the piled up papers covered with writing large and inky. There are bottles filled with brightly coloured liquids with smells to make your eyes water beside instruments made of glass and cold shining metal, some with sharp ends and blades like teeth, and something else floats in the air and up into your nose, not the medicine, not the ink, but always in the air the rich odour of feathers, and there you can see the display cases filled with eggs of the prettiest blues and others that are speckled as though they had been painted. And there in the middle of the huge desk is the big glassy eye of a magnifying glass.

Suddenly, footsteps along the path, heavy but fast, and then squeak of the old garden gate. A man carrying a brown leather bag, well dressed in an overcoat and hat. He walks quickly through the garden; he doesn't stop to take in the air, the scent of honeysuckle or to listen to the birds, for he has other things to think about. Could it be that he is a doctor and the bag is filled with more clinking bottles of sour-tasting medicine. His face is lost in thought, is he is thinking about a patient? Perhaps it is a sick child or perhaps he is worried that he has given the wrong treatment. The front door is opened and he sweeps through the hall; in one movement he hands over his bag and his coat. Then, he stops in front of the grandfather clock, he takes out his watch and looks, the clock is never wrong, he is late. The patient will continue to be in his thoughts as the study door is opened, clicks shut again and he sits down among the bottles and the books.

3b

Monologue: Somewhere in creation

Edward Jenner

In some ways, it seems like yesterday and in others a lifetime ago, but I recall the first time I myself saw a case of small pox. What an impression it made on me and what curiosity and compassion I felt. I was with my brother Stephen, a vicar as our father had been, when I saw the figure of a lady stepping into a carriage. My eye had been caught by the splendour of the carriage and the beauty of the horses before it. The lady held her head low and her hood was down, but as she sat inside, she pulled back the hood, a relief no doubt on such a warm day. It was then I saw and I could not help but stare. The surface of her face was a mass of small crater-like scars, there seemed no part that was not pitted and broken. The scars though small were deep and, though the effect was shocking, my curiosity was greater than my horror. The face so cruelly marked was framed by rich dark curls worn loose beneath her hood and I imagined her once beautiful. I came to learn that the small pox is no respecter of rank or money. It attacks rich and poor alike. Yet, there were differences, too; a lady as the one I had seen in that day could be affected, but the milk maids around my village home always seemed to have skin like the milk in their pails, creamy, full and white. The milk maids never seemed to succumb to the terrible pox.

After my schooling was done and my apprenticeship to surgery served, I went to London to further my studies in medicine, but afterwards, I wished to return to my home village of Berkeley. Here I could study nature, but my thoughts returned to the dreadful and frequently deadly disease that had so haunted my mind, the small pox. I looked around at nature, so generous, so abundant and I began to believe that the answer was somewhere in creation. Nature would not allow us to suffer without providing somewhere a cure.

In common with other physicians, I had used the practice of 'variolation' that is 'injecting' a microscopic amount of the pus taken from small pox pustules into the patient, so as to protect them from contracting the disease in full. However, this was never satisfactory or reliable and my own thoughts turned to the world around me. I thought again of the milk maids and how, though blessed with fair faces, they were always afflicted with the rough blisters of the cow pox on their hands. Could it be that in being affected by the cow pox, nature was protecting them from a worse fate, the small pox itself? Moreover, could it be possible that this protection from small pox could be shared by others, by giving them a dose of the blister pus from cow pox? In my mind, I could hear the words of my teachers in London: 'Don't think, try.' So, I did.

My notion was to introduce fluid from the fresh pustules of cow pox into the body of a patient. This patient must have neither suffered from cow pox or small pox in the past. In my own part of the world I found the very persons needed. Little Sarah Nelmes, a girl of a local family, had on her finger the cow pox blister; from her I could take the fluid. Next, upon enquiry, I discovered the son of my own gardener to be the ideal subject to receive the cow pox fluid. The boy, young James Phipps, had never been afflicted with either the cow pox or the small pox. First I made small cuts in his arm and into them I placed the pus fluid. I did not bother the boy with the learning of what I did, for I could not expect him or his parents to understand. After receiving the cow pox fluid he sickened, the cow pox blisters came, but soon he was recovered. Then, I followed the logic of my experiment; using a sharp lance I injected the boy with a minute sample of pus from a sufferer of small pox. The following days were the most anxious of my life. I enquired constantly after his health and was most eager to inspect his face where the small pox pustules first appear. However, to my great relief he never caught the small pox. Heartened by this result, I repeated the experiment on the boy, but still he did not get the small pox. My hypothesis was correct and I was elated, the task now was to convince others.

It did not concern me that some people said what I did was against nature, that it was disgusting to use the disease of an animal in human beings. To my mind what was truly disgusting was to see infants dying and disfigured in front of their helpless parents. I also ignored the infamous sketch showing a man with a cow's head after he had been treated by me. Though I will admit, the one thing that did cause me distress were the whisperings of my own neighbours, the talk that I took advantage of my position and that the Phipps family had no choice but to agree to James's treatment: 'they daren't say no to Dr. Jenner.' Of course none of this was ever said to my face, but some of the wild talk was repeated to me by servants. There was even sour talk that I had given the Phipps family money, so that I could conduct experiments on the boy.

There were setbacks, of course. As my treatment was taken up by others, a confusion between the cow pox fluid and that of small pox led to mistakes, but gradually many lives were saved. It was said to me that had I kept the secret of this 'miracle' to myself, I could have made my fortune, but instead I built a hut in my own garden where persons of every means could be given free of charge the treatment to protect them against the small pox. For myself, I have the satisfaction of knowing that I have played some small part in helping my fellow men.

If I may say . . . something I have long treasured, a letter from Mr Thomas Jefferson, president of what is called the United States of America. (Clears throat, to read the letter): 'Sir, I avail myself of this occasion of rendering you a portion of the tribute of gratitude due to you from the whole human family.' I must admit, I was most flattered – these colonials have a pleasant way of expressing themselves.

4

Monologue: Products from peanuts

George Washington Carver

A scientist is leaning over to read what is inscribed on the stone in front of him.

'He could have added fortune to fame but, caring for neither, he found happiness and honour in being helpful to the world.' Well, I suppose as tombstones go, a person could have worse said about them. At the end, the only question worth asking about a person is, 'Did they do any good?' and I guess they think I did . . . Sorry, did I say? This tombstone is mine.

Now, it strikes me as a pity, whenever there is a monument to anyone, it always shows their face and not their hands. After all, it's the hands that do the work and God never made finer tools than these hands of ours. I wouldn't call mine pretty but they certainly loved to work and not just on the land. When I first went to college, they set me on painting and playing piano, it was that sort of place and I was happy just to be there. The art came easy, that's what I always did; draw the plants and flowers around the home place. Of course, later I moved on to where I could really study the soil and how to capture its goodness.

I fought for my education, too, and I earned every cent to pay for it, working whatever jobs I could get, from farm hand to cook. But, there was one thing that I learned for free, something that anyone who has ever known poverty recognises, a real empty belly or 'dust again for dinner' also knows how to make a lot out of a little. That's what I wanted the black farmers, no . . . all farmers scraping a living in the south to realise; there are ways of getting more from the land. When I wrote about my ideas in my book *Help for Hard Times*, many people questioned who would listen to the son of a slave, and a man who had been a slave himself. But, it seemed to me that the whole of the south was a slave, a slave to growing cotton. Cotton takes out all the goodness, but other crops replace the nitrogen and put the goodness back, crops like peanuts and sweet potatoes. So I loaded up my wagon and I travelled around to tell people how to rotate the cropping to keep the land from being sucked dry. What I wanted was a way to freedom, a way for people to earn a living from the land without bleeding it so dry that in the end it could give no more.

Well, many did as I advised them and I can't say I blame them for getting a little agitated at the stockpiles of peanuts that they couldn't eat or sell. So, it was time to think deeper still and find other ways to use up the crop. And I always said; if you love a thing, it will give up its secrets to you and that is so. Nature told me some of her secrets in the laboratory, and others she whispered in the fields, and by the end we had around three hundred products and uses derived from the peanut. I do hope you can taste my hard work in your peanut butter, but there were also oils, ink, cosmetics, glue . . . nothing was wasted. The earth wasn't made with garbage dumps; nature has a use for everything, it's people who waste. There were also one hundred uses found for the sweet potato and seventy-five for the pecan nut. There it is, what science can give us are practical ways to discover what nature can do for us. Can you use it? Could somebody else use it? Can it make life better and more decent? It was pointed out to me on more than one occasion, that I could have been a rich man with all of my discoveries. But God gave me those things, how can I charge others for them? Yes, if I must have a tombstone at all, then I'm pleased to have this one.

5

Monologue: Wrinkled peas

Gregor Mendel

In the garden of an Augustan Monastery, a brother is planting seeds. He continues to work as he speaks.

Who do you look like, your father or your mother . . . or maybe it's someone else in the family, perhaps someone you've never even met? Forgive me, but I'm sure that you must have been told who you take after. The day we're born there are faces looking into the cradle: 'He's got his mother's eyes' or 'that's her mother's chin, definitely the chin.' Sometimes people see what they want to see to believe that they are passing part of themselves on to the next generation. After all, we have known since Adam and Eve that human beings are full of pride.

It's not surprising we are proud; like everyone else, when I was a small child I was taught that God made human beings to be special, he saved us until last. Yet, I have come to know by working here in this garden at this monastery that human beings may be God's special creatures, but they pass on characteristics from parent to offspring in the same way as the plants and animals, through what you will call their genes. That is, each parent gives a part of themselves for each feature, such as eye colour or the shape of the nose, but though the parents create the new life together, their genes do not mix, they are passed on unchanged, remaining stubbornly themselves. There is a battle raging to see which genes will win through. Even in this quiet garden the battle goes on with the plants I grow.

Perhaps because I do God's work as a monk, he also helps me and has given me the most wonderful assistants for my experience, these humble pea plants. These pea plants produce two generations each year, they contain both male and female reproductive parts and can either self seed or breed with others. As if they hadn't given me enough, when the experiment is over, I can eat them! As I bred the different varieties of peas, I observed the results of their reproduction in their offspring from the first generation to the next and so on. I could see how each part of the plant inherited traits from the parents, the shape of pod, the seed colour and so on. The features that I speak of were never a mixture of both parents, but always passed on by one or the other.

You may ask, what has all this got to do with a monk? I myself will never marry or pass on any features to children; wouldn't I be better spending my time praying? But, I am a farmer's son and I have seen how crops and cattle are bred and cross bred with the healthiest specimens to produce the fattest and the best. Not that I wished to stay on the family farm, I wanted most to continue with my education, which is why I came to the monastery and to serve God, of course.

Growing up on the farm taught me that nature could be cruel, but I have come to know that it can also be merciful and full of second chances. As I moved the plants around the monastery, I noticed how they were affected by changes of light and temperature and yet the offspring of these plants were undamaged by what the parent plants experienced. And what is more, just because a characteristic doesn't show up immediately in the offspring, it doesn't mean that it won't appear later in a future generation, a gene carried through and suddenly dominant, like an echo of the past.

So, now I must be about my work and the next time you are asked who it is you take after, I hope you will you will think most carefully before you answer.

Monologue: A light at the end of the tunnel

Humphry Davy

The scientist is hunched over the laboratory bench.

When I was young, there was a man who used to walk about our town as if in a daze. It was said that he could not sleep, or rather that he would not allow himself to sleep for fear of nightmares. Years before, he had heard the dreadful blast of an explosion in a nearby mine and later helped to dig and pull out all the dead and injured they could find, those poor broken bodies.

You see, I grew up in the county of Cornwall, a place where mining the rich reserves of tin under the earth was a way of life for many people, but so was the terrible fear of accidents in those mines. When I began my own work, I determined to do something to help stop the suffering caused by these accidents; after all, what is the point of learning anything if you cannot help others by it? I began by knowing that the miners must have some light to see in the pitch darkness; however, it was that very light, the candles that they carried, which both helped the miners and destroyed them. For it was the sparks from those candle flames that ignited the underground gases and caused many blasts. We could do nothing about the gases, they would always be present, and therefore, it occurred to me to create a barrier between those gases and the flames.

I worked the matter through by encasing the flame in a wire gauze and then in a glass cylinder. So now the light could shine through to brighten the darkness and show the miner his way, but no spark could escape into the darkness to ignite the gases. My lamp was a success; more lives saved and fewer widows and orphans. They gave me a pension as thanks for my work, but the money did not matter so much to me; many were surprised that I did not try to grab every penny I could for my invention. No, to my mind, if a man finds a thing that may help others, he is wrong to keep it to himself. After all, an artist or a poet – and I know many poets – cannot keep their work to themselves, they always wish to share it with the world.

It was the same with the nitrous oxide vapour, a most miraculous substance able to relieve pain of all kinds, from a toothache to cramps in the stomach. There were many, including myself, who took the vapour to enjoy the wild joy that inhaling it spreads through the body. How can I explain it to you? Have you ever laughed until your face ached and your sides hurt, but you could not say what has made you laugh so? That is how it is taking the nitrous oxide, and often in rooms with other people equally shaken with uncontrolled mirth. And why not bring about laughter through science? If we cannot make life a little better for each other, what good are we at all?

Monologue: Is it a mad man in the mirror?

Ibn Al-Haytham

The scientist is seated on the floor holding a dust covered mirror. He traces a line delicately with his finger in the dust and then blows the dust into the air.

Even dust can be beautiful in the sunlight, see how it dances in its golden prison, until it falls and is forgotten? Will I also be forgotten, here in the darkness of my prison? Would you believe that I was once a famous man and a trusted servant to the great Caliph? Now I live in darkness, stripped of all my possessions, mocked and hated as a madman.

But, believe me, it is far better that the Caliph should believe that I am mad, for if he was to learn the truth, that I am in my right mind and that I only pretend to be mad, he would have my head, for sure. You see, I came to this land to serve the Caliph, to use my skills to fulfil his scheme to change the path of the great River Nile. But then, as I understand the problem, I realise that it is not possible to change the river's course. But, now, you tell me, in my place, would you say to the Caliph: 'Sire, great one, it . . . it . . . it is not possible.' For you know, he will say 'It must be so, if I wish it!' Great men cannot be disappointed, if we disappoint them, then we must pay with our lives. So, I pretend to be mad, in the hope that he will not hurt a man who appears to have lost his mind.

Yet, here in my prison, at least my mind is free. At least I can pursue my work and my true interest. I seek to know the true nature of light, to discover its source, its power and by what means it travels. Is it possible, that we ordinary men can decide where it may and may not shine? I think about the single ray of light coming into my cell. Must it always shine in the same place or may the light be sent to another part of the room. I wonder what will happen if I shine the bright gaze of a mirror against it, if I make the light look at itself? What will happen then? So, I ask my guards for a mirror; they are not sure at first, they look at each other. Then I whisper, 'I want to see the madman'. And they laugh, I make them laugh and they bring me what I ask.

I have lost my freedom but I am able to think and to learn. I am given all I need for my work. That is, guards who see no harm in indulging the wishes of a man without his wits bring me whatever I ask. For example, I ask them to hang the lanterns outside my room at different heights. Now I see in the short time that my door is opened, from each lantern a spot of light cast on my wall. The faint little spot at the highest level, can be traced back to the lantern hung at the highest point, while the spot of light lower down the wall, I see comes from the lantern hung lower down. Then, I call out for each lantern in turn to be covered and I see the spot of light that it cast also disappears. Now, I see that it is not as the ancient men have told us, that it is not the fire in our eyes that lights up the world; if that were true, it wouldn't matter if the lantern was covered, we should still be able to see. I realise that light, in fact, comes into our eyes from a source and when that source is covered, so its light disappears and can no longer enter our eyes and be seen. I try this many times with the lanterns, moving them around, covering and uncovering them. I see for myself by trying, by demonstrating that it is indeed true.

Now, a last secret for you, I tell you truly: knowledge also is a light, it helps us to see the world clearly and it is this beautiful light of knowledge that shines brightest of all.

8

Monologue: Reflecting on the scientist cleaning up nursing

Joseph Lister

A young woman in a nurse's uniform is pulling sheets off a bed and making a bundle with them.

I'm not talking to Ethel, she just can't help making nasty remarks. I'd rushed home from the hospital because my sister Rose had said she'd got something to tell us. Well, I was so happy when she said that she was getting married, I threw my hands up to my face. That was when Ethel opened her big mouth: 'You'll never get a ring on your finger with hands like that!' she says, laughing. Well, I looked at my hands all red and swollen and thought, she's right. It's all his fault, 'Dr Germs'. He has us scrubbing morning till night. Well, he never actually talks to us, it's matron who gives the orders. But you can smell him coming before he's even there, stinks of the carbolic soap, he does. Still, you can't argue with the facts, less people are dying after their operations.

They say he got his ideas about killing off infection from a Frenchman. This Frenchman said he'd found these tiny little dots of things, which he called bacteria, growing. That's when the doctor here thought it might be these bacteria growing on wounds, infecting them and causing the patients to die. Before that, they'd always thought that it was the bad air causing the infection. Made sense to me; all that sickness is bound to make the air bad, stands to reason. When you work in a hospital, it's the smell of sickness you have to get used to first and then you don't notice it after a bit. Smells a bit different here, though, from the hospital I was at, it's all that strong carbolic acid soap you can smell here.

The doctor thought that if you could kill off the bacteria, you could stop the infection. He started off with broken bones: if the bone stayed under the skin, you could just plaster round and that was all right. But, if the bone came through the skin, the wound was terrible; most died of that, but the doctor tried cleaning these wounds with carbolic and it seemed to make the difference, enough to convince him, anyway. Now, everything is scrubbed clean, all the instruments, bedding, everything going near the patient.

I got the idea about being a nurse when gran died. She went to have her appendix out, said she'd see me on Sunday for church, but she died just two days after they opened her up. The wound had turned black, it was that bad. Our Rose always says to me, 'I don't know how you can look at all those disgusting diseases'. But it doesn't bother me. I told gran that I'd look after her, but I never got the chance. I wish gran had her operation here, it might have saved her.

They come from all over to talk to him, the doctor, 'the great surgeon', to get his opinion on things. Don't know why you'd want to look at his hairy face, unless you had to. Well, better get on, matron will be coming on her inspection soon, looking out for spots of dirt on our aprons and at our hands front and back. She's been even more particular than usual; they think the poor old girl who was in this bed died of an infection. You'd think the germs'd be scared of matron, everybody else is. Still, you can't stop every bit of dirt, much as the doctor would like to. The used sheets here will get burned not washed, seems like a waste, but doctor's orders and it'll save my hands.

9

Monologue: Artistry and science

Leonardo Da Vinci

How did you get in here? I heard no footsteps, though to be truthful when the church bells are ringing it would be impossible to hear a lion roar, let alone a few small feet. I suppose the boys left the door open again; they are always . . . oh, I'm sorry, the boys? My apprentices of course. I let them go early, after all, they have worked hard. All of the day they have been preparing the paint, grinding the colours, mixing the yolk of eggs to bind the paint, whilst others with their sleeves rolled up were rubbing down the wooden panels to prepare them for the paint. I cannot complain, I was an apprentice myself for six years, I understand they want to run out and be free sometimes.

Wait a moment! Has the Duke sent you? Well, go back and tell his highness that I apologise with all my heart and that he shall have the painting when it is finished. I could not give such a great man a half finished painting could I? Although, it can't be tomorrow, tomorrow I have other things to do. I have an appointment with a surgeon. No, not for me, I am in good health, but I shall be observing the cutting open of someone not so fortunate, a dead body. Since my earliest days, I have made a study of the human body, to observe how the muscle is bound to the bone, the finest sculpture and the ligaments strung like the finest musical instruments. To truly understand the beauty of how it works, we must pull back the skin and look closely at the skeleton, how it truly is.

Yes, the painter needs to understand nature and how it works and nature needs the painter to show it in all its glory and strangeness, too. They work together, they are the greatest friends, and we should not try to keep them apart. Now if you will excuse me . . . where was I? Oh yes, yes, I must put down a few drawings, an idea that came to me in a dream. In this dream, I was out in the fields near my father's house, where I spent so much time drawing the flowers and plants when I was young. Suddenly, I was lifted into the air and floated above the flowers. It was so real that I jolted awake as though I had fallen from the sky. But, how exciting it was! And I began to think, what if a man could fly, how would it change his view of creation of the world? For once you have tasted flight, you will walk the earth with your eyes turned skyward, for there you have been and there you will long to return. Now, I must begin to put down my ideas, my own machine of the air. Let yourselves out.

10

Discussion between two scientists: A lock without a key

Luigi Galvani and Alessandro Volta

Two scientists are standing as though in a doorway discussing their work.

Volta: After you, sir.
Galvani: No, please, my friend, go on.
Volta: I insist . . .
Galvani: Very well, then.

They enter, Galvani first, followed by Volta. They look at the people in front of them.

Galvani: An audience! I'm flattered.
Volta: No more than you deserve, no more than you deserve.
Galvani: Nor you, my friend.
Volta: I suppose they are here for us?
Galvani: Of course! See how excited they are, how eager to listen. Especially this one at the front and him over there.
Volta: It's just electricity . . . it's so . . .
Galvani: Difficult?
Volta: No, not difficult, it's they know so much about everything!
Galvani: They don't know about us, they don't know about 'our' electricity.
Volta: True.
Galvani: They don't know how it all started, what we did, what we found.
Volta: Shall I begin?
Galvani: Please do. I'll just listen, I won't interfere.

Volta:	Thank—
Galvani:	Or interrupt. Not a word . . .
Volta:	Thank you! I'll begin by telling you a little about myself. As the emperor, once said to me . . .

Galvani is coughing loudly.

Volta:	Is there something wrong?
Galvani:	I was only thinking these children might like to hear about our work, while they are still young.
Volta:	I was getting to it!
Galvani:	Allow me. Let us start at the beginning. As a doctor, I studied the body. I discovered that the nerves of the body are charged with the force to make muscles move, the force of animal electricity—
Volta:	That is where I cannot agree, there is no 'animal electricity.' Let me explain—
Galvani:	You'll get your chance. I know how you like to 'entertain' the public.
Volta:	I gave scientific demonstrations on the force of electricity on the body.
Galvani:	And what about the force of the body's electricity?

They begin to speak simultaneously.

Volta:	I never said that there weren't muscle spasms in the animals that you observed, simply that it was the actions of the metals in contact with the body that caused the movement spasm.
Galvani:	I observed for myself the muscle spasm in the legs of creatures now dead, it must have been an energy stored in the muscle's 'animal electricity' . . . STOP! This won't do.
Volta:	Nothing was ever learned by shouting.
Galvani:	Undignified.

They look into the audience.

Volta:	So, shall we?
Galvani:	You take this half and I'll start here.
Volta:	Ready!
Galvani:	Ready!

They gather their half of the audience in a group around them. The group with Galvani hear his speech first and the group with Volta, his.

Galvani:	First, I would like for you to know that I have the greatest respect for my Signore Volta. [*He waves to him.*] But, everything I tell you I have seen with my own eyes and conducted experiments many times over. It began when I was dissecting the legs of a frog. The legs were held in place by brass hooks and when the hooks were touched,

accidentally at first by the steel of my scalpel, the legs twitched! I was struck and repeated what had happened on other animal specimens. The touch had activated the animal electricity within the creature! The force is sent as a liquid from the brain; it penetrates the nerves and muscles and can be stored there, waiting to be activated. It is true, I would agree with him, with my colleague, my friend, the famous Volta, that different metals cause different kinds of muscle spasm. This force is held within every living creature, how else are we moved to action? This force of animal electricity is held within all creatures. After my observations of the frog, I submitted many kinds of animal specimen to the touch of metal on exposed nerve tissue and each time the same, whether a cat, a sheep or a chicken, there was a movement, a jolt, small, yes, but still there. All life holds within it, this force waiting to be released into action.

The scientists wait for each other to finish, they bow cordially as they cross to speak to the other group.

Volta: First, I would like you to know that I have the greatest respect for the good Doctor Galvani. [*He waves to him.*] I would be the first to admit that it was his experiments that inspired me to look further into the force of electricity. No one before the great Doctor Galvani had put together the connection between electricity and movement. He had observed the legs of a frog, pinned down by brass hooks as he dissected it with a steel scalpel, twitch when the nerves came into contact with metals. He said it was the electricity stored in the body that caused the twitching, but I said no! I felt that it was not so. It was, rather, the metals themselves, the electrical charge created by the steel of the scalpel and the brass of the hooks, that sent a shock into the animal's body. I made my own experiments with metals and I started here. [*He sticks out his tongue and points to it.*] Never, ignore what is in front of you and, as you see, a tongue can always be in front of you. I began by placing a silver spoon and a piece of tin, connected by a copper wire, on my tongue. There was a tingle on my tongue, unmistakable. I knew that it was the action of the metals when drawn together by the wire that was creating this tingle, this 'shock'. I wanted to make the experiment bigger, so I built a tower of metal discs, zinc and silver, and connected the top and bottom of the tower with a copper wire. Between the discs I put a cloth soaked in salty water, I thought this salt water could replace the bitter juices of my own mouth. This is what you would call a battery. I had bound together metals with a wire to conduct the force between them and bathed by an acid liquid. The more metal discs

I added, the stronger the force and if I took some away, the force grew weaker. I had proved, at least to myself, that it is the metals themselves when drawn together by a conductor—

Galvani: I hope my colleague has not confused you.
Volta: I hope my colleague has not tired you.

They may indicate that they should swap groups or they may ask the class to find a partner from the opposing group to tell them something that they remember from the speech they heard.

Galvani: So, we had our say.
Volta: Yes, indeed.
Volta: They are the two sides to the story.
Galvani: Just what I was going to say!
Volta: Shall we go?

They go to leave together.

Volta: After you, sir
Galvani: No, please my friend, go on
Volta: I *insist* . . .

They exit.

11a

Monologue: A shillin' on the shore

Mary Anning

A well dressed stranger is skimming the sand with his stick, as a young girl cleans off an ammonite fossil with her small muddy hands.

I seen you lookin', is it the ammo you want? I seen you lookin', you won't get nothin' just poking your stick to and fro, you needs to get your 'ands dirty, see? Tide'll be in soon, sea's swellin' up, I feel it. Won't get no more finding done today . . . best take this 'un . . . a shillin'. I'll shine it up good, too, the visitors like them nice to take back to London, show their friends, this 'un's a good one for showin'. That's where they mostly come from, London, come here for the good air, sea air, good for the health, they say. Well, so's eatin' good for the health and a shillin' will put bread in the mouth, no trouble.

Got a bit before the tide comes, see this 'un's scraping up nice. You from London, then? One day, I should like to see London or somesuch, Exeter maybe. I heard they got places with things dug up, all in cases, just to look at, like, can't imagine things just to look at, things is for usin' . . . or for sellin', don't care what folks do with 'em after that. I should think my father would have done well there; he made cabinets, things to put other things in. He be gone now, gone two year ago, couldn't leave us nothin' but debt, no bread for us nor the baby in mother's belly. Only thing he could leave to me and Joe was how well he knew this shore. He knew where the creatures and monsters were hid, brought us up 'ere at low tide to find bones in the cliff, ever since we were babes ourselves.

Mother frets when we do come 'ere to hunt for the bones and the curiosities, but she do mind less when we brings back money, too. Joe's been hunting further up today, we split up, find more that way. He's good too, Joe, he'd be better if he had more stomach for it like me. Only time I ever saw 'im excited was when he found the fish monster. It were like he seen a ghost and I suppose he had. Story went that I found it, but it were Joe, though I did dig and prise parts from the rock, so we be square on that. Eighteen feet long it were, by the time we got it out. Everyone come to see, ichthyosaurus, they said it be, fetched a pretty penny too, by the time we put it right and laid it in a case with cement. I put it all together, there I am better than Joe, I just know how a creature should look, where the bones belong and what they be. One of them clever men what came to see it, he asked me, 'Child, how do you know to recognise these bones?' I says, 'Can't say, sir'. He says, 'How do you know to which species they belong?' I says, 'Can't say, sir'. Then he says, 'it must truly be a gift' and I says, 'Can't say, sir'. Then he walks off. I should have mentioned my father learning me, I suppose, but somehow, it just feels as natural to me to know them bones and fossils, like people recognising their own kin, I just know, maybe I was born knowin'. And, I know from books I seen, if they have it right or wrong, too, even thinkin' men what wrote them.

Tide's comin' now; we don't want to get cut off. The sea's master here, it'll wash out more fossils when it feels like it, or wash us in, it don't care. Maybe that's why father never worried about sendin' us out, he knew I wouldn't try to cheat the sea. 'You'll be all right', he said, 'the Annings always are'. See, sir, said I'd make it shine, worth a shillin' now. Better move now. I'll be back at low tide, you want more, I be here, I always be here.

11b

Discussion between the young scientist and older people: Lyme Regis (on the seashore) in 1809

A lady and gentleman visiting from London are walking along the sea shore. They are pointing out shells to each other in the sand and pick up one to look at. A young local girl (dressed in a bonnet and rather ragged clothing) runs over to them.

Mary:	Please sir, I can find you something better than that. See sir, it's an ammo!
Lady:	An ammo? What is an ammo?
Mary:	An ammonite ma'am. They're what remains of the long ago sea creatures.
Gentleman:	Oh, yes. There are plenty of them around here. We have been offered so many of them to buy.
Mary:	Not like this one sir, I bet the others will be smaller.
Lady:	I'm not sure. There are a lot of them in the sand.
Mary:	See the beautiful spiral pattern and hard like bone.
Gentleman:	You are a very determined young lady.
Lady:	I suppose it would be nice for our collection.
Mary:	No one better than me at digging out the treasures from the sand and the rocks.
Gentleman:	How much do you want for it?
Mary:	Well, they are worth a lot of money. But, I'll take a penny.

They hand over the money and Mary runs off, pleased.

12

Monologue: Where does the river go?

Rachel Carson

Shh . . . did you hear that? Wrens outside on the cherry tree . . . to be so small and yet have so much to say . . . I guess that's what they thought about me when I was a little girl. You know, one of the first stories I ever wrote . . . maybe I was the same age as you . . . was called 'Mr Wren and Jenny Wren Find a Home'. I just loved to watch them with their tails stuck out, so proud of their nests, their place. The story got put into a magazine, too . . . mamma was so proud. You see, I knew, I just knew that I would be a writer, but later when I studied science, everyone would say, 'So, you gonna be a scientist or a writer, you can't be both, you know'. Well, why not? Do you like stories and science, I do! I was lucky in that the place I grew up in gave me plenty of inspiration for stories. I can see it now, I'm five years old with my mother; we're walking the woods behind our house. Her arms are full of baskets of all the things we've picked and collected. Her hands are full, so I hold on to her skirt and trail along. We name every flower, every bird and every tree. Mamma taught me to look and she would say, 'Rachel, do you know the name of the river?' I'd say 'Yes, mamma', and ask; 'but where does the river go?' Questions, always questions, I guess that's what makes a scientist.

Many years later when I wrote my book, *Silent Spring*, I wanted to tell people a story, the story of nature, how it works, why we should take care what we do with it. It was sort of like nature was the main character in the story. I wanted people to read it and understand more about the world around us. But then, because ordinary people could read and understand it, they said it just wasn't scientific enough. But you see, nature is a story, it's really the story of us, how we have been formed by our environment; the food it gives us, the climate, the dangers and how we survived.

I'm afraid that children nowadays, just won't get the chance to enjoy nature as I did, children like my own boy, Roger. What kind of a world will he grow up in? What will there be left to enjoy, when we finish poisoning the land and the water with weed killers? That's really why I wrote *Silent Spring*. You see I thought that if people knew about the chemicals, they would care, they would want it to stop. *Silent Spring*, that was a strange title! My life was far from silent. The people at the chemical companies, other scientists, said I had my facts wrong, that I was exaggerating and without weed killer and insecticides, the crops would fail and we would starve. They said that I listened too much to 'ordinary folks', people who noticed that birds stopped coming to their gardens, that they got rashes or felt ill after chemicals were sprayed nearby.

It's like, have you ever held hands in a circle? Whatever you pass around, always comes back to you. That's why when we harm living things, we are just harming ourselves. It's true, I did say 'I am pessimistic about mankind'. I can't help it. The trouble is, we don't let nature itself help us, we work against it and eventually it fights back. Of course if you only plant one kind of crop because that crop makes you more money, the insects that like to eat that crop will thrive. We need different crops; difference is good, what we call diversity. It means that different insect populations grow up and they control each other in their own natural wars for survival. When we spray with poisons, we don't just kill what we call the 'pests' themselves, but all the other creatures that could have helped us to control them. Then, we make matters worse by killing and killing until the insects become resistant and the next generation become even more powerful against us. Bugs, they can survive almost anything!

Worst of all, the chemicals get into our own food supply: cows eat grass sprayed with weed killer, it gets into their milk; did you know that DDT has been found in baby teeth? DDT. Yes, that's what I said. Let me explain, DDT is a chemical insect killer, it belongs to a family of chemicals called... now here's a scientific term for you, chlorinated hydrocarbons... Say it ... Chlorin-ated hydro-carbons. Chlorin-ated. Hydro-carbons. Sound like a tongue twister? I have always loved words, but these words leave a nasty taste in the mouth. Just remember the last part, carbon. It's the very element that we and all other living creatures are based on. Carbon is a true force of nature, it can dance its way into so many different shapes and patterns, that's why we have so many different kinds of life, from tiny fleas to the blue whale and us. But carbon makes friends easily, too. It can link easily with other elements to form new compounds. This is why carbon is so useful to produce the different chemical sprays that we turn on nature. Human beings, so clever, I guess that's how we survived, but that very cleverness could also be our own downfall.

The trouble is, it can take a long time to notice these changes happening, like the bugs eating the bark from a tree that has been sprayed to kill Dutch Elm disease, the worms eating the bugs, the birds eating the worms and although the birds may not actually die, they may produce less young, fewer chicks.

I bet people tell you all the time to listen, your teachers, your parents, so I promise to say it just once, if you'll promise to listen. If you don't learn to hear nature speaking to us through bird song, if you don't know what ought be there and how what we humans do can so easily change it, you may not even notice, when finally there is a silent spring.

13

Monologue: Full stretch

Joseph Shivers

You haven't seen me . . . I'm not supposed to be here, they think I'm in the laboratory. I just came out for a minute to check the score, now I wish I hadn't. Last time I looked they were winning, now . . . well, how did that happen?

You like sport? You play? You watch? Let me ask you this, when you're running or jumping or kicking a ball in your school yard or in the garden or even watching a game on TV, do you ever imagine that you're somewhere else and there's a crowd cheering for you? Well, maybe someday there will be a crowd cheering just for you. Oh, and one more question; excuse me, I love questions: do you know what it is you need to be a winner or part of a winning team? Well, talent, yes of course, but mainly, it's stamina. You know what that is? No? Well, ask your teacher! No, I'm kidding, I'll tell you what stamina is: it's being able to keep going and keep trying and not get upset when things go badly for you. Oh no, I'm not a sportsman, no I'm a scientist. Although, it is similar, there were times when I certainly needed stamina to carry on, when it seemed that I would never get the right answer. But, unlike most sportsmen, I was lucky that I could choose my own team. Speaking of teams, when I watch sports, I sometimes feel that I'm part of the team, after all, it was the work I did that found the material that most athletes have in their clothing. The stuff I discovered is the substance that gives the material its stretch and allows the clothes to get back into shape, no matter how much they get used. Of course, in the beginning, we didn't use the material for sports; no it was, well, if you must know, it was for underwear! And not just anybody's underwear either, it was for the stars! Not the ones up in the sky, that would look plain silly, I'm talking about film stars. We found, that is myself and my team found, the material that could be put into the actors' underwear, the sort of thing they all wore to keep themselves looking all pulled in and slim, to make it more comfortable for them to wear.

By the way, you might want to check the labels on your clothes, I'll bet anything you have some of the material that we discovered in what you're wearing today. The stuff we made makes it easier for you to do all that running, jumping and kicking stuff that we talked about and it keeps your clothes in shape, too. You see, it's like a queue, first we deal with the important people, you know, the movie stars, the sports stars, and then eventually, everyone else gets to use it, too. Yes, I suppose that is a little unfair.

It's like when I was working on a drug to cure malaria; a terrible disease, take it from me. It's hard to understand when you're lucky to live in a country like this, where Malaria isn't a problem. But, in countries with a tropical climate, hot and wet, too, during the rainy season, it causes such pain and misery. But, we didn't start trying to cure malaria to help the poor ordinary people suffering from malaria; no it was to help soldiers fighting in China. After this, slowly but surely, our work and research went on to help cure other people, too. Like I said, it's a queue, only unlike nice stretchy clothes, having to wait for malaria medicine is even more unfair.

And, I'll tell you something else that isn't fair, not being able to sneak out for a few minutes to check the score without someone coming to look for you. Oh well, the way they're playing, I'm not sure I want to look anyway.

14

Monologue: Tiny island, big sea

Marianne North

Rain, rain, rain, rain. That's what seems to rule this country, the rain! You think about all the things it stops you from doing. No playing outside, no going to meet friends or going walking. I've met my share of rulers and important men and not one single one of them kept me waiting as long as the rain. I am sorry to be bad tempered, I know that they are just concerned about my health and going out while it is so wet. I admit, before I left England, I never knew any discomfort at all. That is why everyone was so surprised when they learned of my travels. The hours I spent trudging across rough tracks, scouring cliff edges and wading through rivers, all by mule with irritating insects and wasps biting at me.

When my father died, I had my own money and I was free to go wherever I chose, and I chose far, far away. We are a tiny island on a big sea and I wanted to find out what was across that sea. What wonders of nature would await me? Unusual plants, flowers and trees had always fascinated me. But I could never in my wildest imagination have dreamt of the glories I found in the lush hidden forests of the Americas, the rare flowers of Ceylon and the fruits of the Caribbean.

The rain here is not like the rain you see in the tropics, that is for certain. There it is like the tears of a million angels and when it stops all the sadness is washed away and the colours sing for joy. We need to invent new words to describe these colours. I shall never forget the burning amber of the wild orchids of South America, the lush green of the feather-like branches leading to the Taj Mahal and the blood red glow of a South American poinsettia. But what I have brought back from my travels is perfect. Nothing has been plucked or taken from its home. These plants and flowers live on in my imagination and in my paintings. It is true that you must you see these wonders for yourself to truly know why the colours are worth trekking up mountains to see, but I hope I have done a fair job describing them in my work.

And if you are ever visiting Kew Gardens, I hope you will see my paintings exhibited there, that is if this rain ever stops and we can finally take them there!

15

Monologue: My son's reflections

Benjamin Franklin

First, I would like to make it plain that I was not a child, when one dark and stormy night I trudged across that field with my father. No sir, I was 21, a grown man, though I was still willing to follow my father everywhere, even in the dark. So please ignore those truly ridiculous drawings of a man and a small boy clutching a kite in the rain, they are hokum and not for smart folks like you.

Not that it matters much; after all, it wasn't always easy to be my father's son at any age. It seemed impossible to go anywhere, without someone saying: 'So, you're the son of the great man.' Yes, scientist, inventor, politician, you name it, my father was it. And it wasn't just the great men he knew either, ordinary people, blacksmiths and bakers admired him just as much. Though, I can imagine, my father being the fifteenth child of seventeen, that he was eager to get out and make a name for himself. First, he was apprenticed to his own brother James who owned a print works. However, things did not go well and my father wound up running away!

However, it was in reading the books and newspapers printed by James, that my father's interest in electricity was first ignited. Reading articles from across Europe detailing the experiments taking place and then attending demonstrations by scientists, the likes of which seemed as much like magic as science. They would have machines to produce static electricity to make a person's hair fly outwards or charge a member of the audience full of static electricity so that to touch him would give an electric shock or if it were a lady, an invitation to kiss her really would be shocking! How could they have known, that sitting in the audience was the brightest spark of all, my father.

It had been believed that electricity was made up of two fluids, like two forces fighting and colliding, which caused the charge. However, my father came to prove that there was but one substance and this substance circulated and flowed on and on. His mind puzzled over so many problems, but there was only ever one solution; to experiment to carry out a practical study of his own. And, it was precisely one of those experiments that brought us out in a rain storm to that field in June 1752. What a strange sight we must have made, except that everyone else had the good sense to be indoors. My father wanted to prove his idea that the electricity contained in lightning was exactly the same force, the same substance as the electricity that made hair stand on end in those stage experiments. He had made the kite with a large silk handkerchief, fearing a paper kite would be destroyed by the rain. Attached to the top of the kite was a metal wire, like a spike going upwards and at the bottom of the string, close to where he held on, was a key, a metal key. Having sent the kite up into the rain clouds, nothing happened for a good long time, and anyone other than Father would have given up. Then suddenly, some of the fibres from the string began to stand on end and Father did something so simple and yet so important: he touched the key with his knuckle and I could see by his expression, the odd smile I knew so well, that he had felt an electric shock. The wire spike had been caught by lightning and had conducted the electrical charge from the lightning down towards the metal key and then when my father touched it, the charge had flowed on into him. My father had been right, the electricity in lightning had behaved in the same way as the electricity generated at the demonstrations; it flowed and could produce a charge that could actually then be felt. You could say that he was shocked but not surprised.

After this, he attached metal spikes to conduct lightning to the roofs of many buildings, including our home. He rigged up a spike encased in glass into one of the chimneys, which was then connected to a series of metal bells inside the house, so that they would ring whenever there was a rainstorm. He believed that electricity could be harnessed for the good of everyone; he never took money for any of his inventions, he only made things that would do his fellow man a good turn. He continued to invent almost until his death, a good thing he invented bi-focal spectacles, the kind that let you read close and see distances. He never faded, but like the lightning he flashed across our skies and was gone.

16

Monologue: Too late!

Michael Faraday

You're early, I'm afraid the demonstration hasn't started yet. That's why you're here isn't it, to hear my talk and see all electrical wonders that you've heard about? If you stay, you might see your friends' hair flying around; my demonstrations of static electricity are very popular. It all suddenly seems a very long time ago, that I was sitting where you are now, waiting to hear the great scientists talk about their work.

While you're here, make yourselves useful, put those books into that case for me, carefully now, a book is a precious thing. Being from a family that did not have the money to buy books or give me an education, I came to treasure each book that came into my hands. Fortunately, some of them stayed in my hands for a long time, as I was apprenticed to a book binder and it was careful and slow work. I had to be precise, no wasting of materials, they cost money. It was a step by step craft that taught me a lot about working my way slowly but surely to the finished product.

Being an apprentice was also a good way to listen to what others had to teach you, to learn from what they already knew. After all, if it wasn't for the scientist Oersted, discovering the power of magnets, I, and of course, my colleagues, may never have explored the connection between magnets and electrical force. If only I had the time now, I could explain it to you; oh well, maybe just briefly: firstly, I made a dish of mercury, often called quicksilver because of the colour and its liquid form, and into this I placed a magnet and then attached a wire to a battery and placed it in the mercury also. Well, the metal wire spun around the magnet, round and round, spinning around the two poles of the magnet, and it was this turning around both poles that caused the electrical charge. A copper coil would have done just as well as the wire, the point is, this charge, when fully developed, would have the power to drive a motor. It was the start of something astonishing, even in your time, everything driven by an electric motor contains magnets. If you don't believe me, when you go home find some appliances with motors and take them apart . . . no, don't do that, I mean, that is what I would do, but you really mustn't. I'm sure there would be a dreadful fuss.

The great thing is not just to have knowledge, but to harness it, to be useful, to take what you have learned and apply it. Something to know is that electricity, despite its power, is actually rather lazy, it always wants to take the easiest route, to just flow. That is why if you touch a loose wire, it will go through you; you're the easiest route and you will soon know about it. Imagine a water pipe flowing happily, then there's a hole in the pipe; the water will take the first, easiest route out, the hole. In creating an electrical circuit, we have a continuous route for the electricity to flow along, and along that route we can place the items that we would like to power, such as bells and lights. Well now, that seems to be everything set out nicely; there will be a crowd arriving for my talk, but you are most welcome to stay.

17a

Monologue: Alone is best to be

Isaac Newton

When I was born, I was so small they did not expect that I would live. I cannot always join in with the rough games that the others boys play, but it's no matter to me, alone is best to be. The moon will be up soon, it always comes back to us. Why does it? No matter how bad we are, it always comes back. I keep a chart of the moon and stars and tomorrow will be the full moon. One day I should like to see the sea, we're a long way from it here. I'd like to watch how the tides obey the moon and change with it. Why do they? If I go back to school, and my uncle says that I should, I could ask the masters, but they could never answer any of the other questions I asked. They said that my mind worked too fast and I was too curious for my age. When I am a man, I shall buy a telescope of my own and I shall not need to ask, for I will find the answers myself. My uncle brings me books; Father left me none, he could not read himself so had no need of them. Grandmother wonders why I waste my time reading, but she is glad if it keeps me from causing a commotion in the house whenever my mother or my stepfather put me in a temper. She says that this land has had enough troubles with the old King dead and the war.

See this pretty windmill? I made it myself, I finished it today. I will put it beside the clock I made. I wanted to show them to Mother, but now I don't think I will, I am not talking to her or my stepfather either. I made the sails and the wheels, see they turn and grind the corn between them. I don't ask for anything, I can make the tools myself. Over the trees I can see the mill where the grain for our village is ground, I wonder what force, what weight of wind it takes to lift and move the sails. How much grain do you think it takes to make one bag of flour? I should like to try these puzzles on the one I have made and then work out how much greater the force would need to be for the big windmill yonder.

I shall stay here till supper time, here in the apple orchard and nobody shall find me. Grandmother has told one of the men to walk over the farm with me tomorrow, to let me see how the crops are faring. They say that you can tell if the corn is ready by the taste. You break off a piece and chew, but I cannot tell, I have no taste for farming at all. If only I could be left alone to sit and read and think about all the wonders of creation.

17b

Monologue: A mother's reflections

Newton's mother

(The children could be asked to reflect after listening to this . . . what do they, know, think they know and imagine about the scientist the mother is describing?)

I remember his birth as clear as the summer sun makes this lake appear. Premature, he could have fit into a quart mug, though never a bother to my mother, she claimed. I missed raising him. I could do little to change the lot I was given, what with his father dying just before the child's birth and all. I found myself a good man, a reverend, Barnabas Smith. I left my son in my mother's capable hands, she never done me wrong in her raising of me.

My little Christmas miracle.

It pains me, even now so close to the end, that he held such enmity towards me and his stepfather. His words will haunt me to my dying day, as soon as that may be. How could he threaten to burn us both, me, his mother, and Barnabas, and the house over us. I hear that he has since repented these words but I don't begrudge him his feelings. Can't have been an easy childhood, if it be anything akin to mine!

This enmity has not held him back. I know no man alive that can rival him in his thinking on the subjects of mathematics, optics and mechanics and gravitation. I was indeed given much pride on hearing that a fellow scholar of his, a Mr Isaac Barrow, had stated that my boy, though being very young, 'is of an extraordinary genius and proficiency in these things'.

Of his achievements my personal favourite be his discovery that light, plain white light, can be split into what he calls a spectrum of colours. I call it beauty and a sign of God's brightness, but this spectrum can then be changed back into white light when the process is reversed. My boy, the genius he is, has put this discovery to practical use and his reflecting telescope is something of a marvel among scholars.

The colours of this light are truly captivating and the sights he has shown me through his reflecting telescope, however magical, pale in comparison with the work completed recently, a document containing what my boy calls the three universal laws of motion. This recently published work, called *The Principia*, has been slighted by others for its similarity to ideas of an Italian scholar named, I think, Galileo. This man, it would seem, had similar views on the notion of movement and I believe that my son has used these ideas to develop an irrefutable explanation for what he believes to be the notion of gravity and friction.

Sitting staring across this pond, on this summer's day, I am happy. My son, Isaac, will be remembered forever for his contributions to society and his beliefs set out in *The Principia* and supported through his mathematical understanding of worlds.

18

Monologue: The most perfect material

William Harbutt

When I was a boy, I was only happy when my hands were busy. I always had a stone to carve with or a piece of charcoal to draw with . . . and I don't suppose I have changed very much. The only thing I've ever liked as much as making things myself is instructing others to do so; not surprising then, to myself or anyone else, that I became an art teacher.

The thing that delighted me the most was clay, to form models with the cool dampened pieces cut from huge slabs in the studio. I loved to carve and to pinch and to shape, but sadly, the clay did not seem to like me quite so much in return. As I worked at it, the clay resisted and fought back, it was hard work, needing strength that not everyone has. Then when finally I got it to do what I wished, it stubbornly stayed that way, dried out and fixed. Many times I or my pupils would return to a piece of work only to find it too hard and dry to continue working with. It seemed a shame that the clay could not be more co-operative. Think of how strong yet springy your hands are, they can bend and flex and return to their shape, but clay dries and forgets what it was.

I began to wonder if there was a way to make the clay easier and friendlier to use. And so, I began to experiment with a variety of substances to add to the clay. I will not pretend that I didn't need help, lugging those sacks of salts and boxes of petroleum jelly to the cellar was work for two people and Bill, an old soldier, was the man to help me. He and I, and sometimes other members of my family, stirred and mixed and used the garden roller to wring out the water from the soft material that was beginning to be made. And now you think that I'm going to tell you what exactly went into it, don't you? Well, you must understand that I need to keep some secrets about the ingredients, I am sure that other manufacturers would love to know! Now, no more clues, but I will tell you, just between ourselves, it is oil based.

Speaking of business, I realised that if my own children were so entertained by a material that was soft to the hand, would never dry out and, like their own imaginations, could change into a different shapes, why wouldn't other children be? This is especially true when colour is added, and I am proud to say that my daughter, Olive, made the suggestion about colour. Of course I sold my invention to serious artists, too: just imagine, a substance so perfect it allows children to play and artists to create as well. Now, I must get along; we leave for New York later this week to find new customers and no doubt I will need to find a few things to keep me busy on the long sea voyage.

19

Dramatic strategies to make sense of the work of a scientist: The Soho cholera outbreak of 1854

Dr John Snow

The aims of these activities are:

- to explore and discuss locations important to the way of life of the people affected by the cholera outbreak;

- to create an intense imaginary and sensory experience reflecting the living conditions of the people affected by the cholera outbreak; and

- to highlight and begin to identify the problems associated with discovering the source of the cholera outbreak.

Mind movie

Everyone in the group closes their eyes as the teacher/leader reads a short movie:

Left or right? Straight on or round that corner? No stranger would find their way around these streets. At least you've got the bells to rely on; the chimes of St. Luke's church are never late. It's six o'clock, so best watch out, don't want to get knocked down by the men rushing out after they finish work at the brewery. Something else you can always rely on, there'll be beer tomorrow and plenty of it. Well, at least for some, I can't see the guardians at the Poland Street workhouse giving it out; you just work or die in there. What's that? Oh yes, the clatter of the little tin pots, kids queuing up at the water pump, there's a slap for anyone who pushes in, too.

Follow the crowds and there's a terrible sound and it's coming from number 40 Broad Street. Look through the dirty window of number 40, there's a woman nursing a baby, the crying sounds more like a wail and it never stops. The woman is all pale and worn out but she keeps on rocking it.

Everyone opens their eyes and the teacher asks the group to recall all of the places and locations that they remember from listening carefully to the piece:

■ the church

■ the workhouse

■ the brewery

■ the water pump

■ 40 Broad Street.

Some of the locations may need some explanation and a discussion of what they are for and what sort of things might happen in there. The class could also talk about what it must have been like to live in a place that had all of the smells, sights and sounds that were suggested and so close together. What else can we imagine about these people's lives and how are their lives different from our own, for example, the need to collect water and the idea of a workhouse?

The sensory journey

When the teacher feels confident that everyone has enough information about each location, several sheets of newspaper are spread out on the floor (for a class of thirty, you could start with fifteen sheets). The teacher asks the group to walk around the room; the children can walk in any direction, but avoid walking on the newspaper. The teacher will then call out a location, such as, 'the workhouse'. When the children hear this, they must quickly find a sheet of newspaper to stand on, which will represent the place. There will be more people than sheets of paper, so the class must share, reflecting the tightly packed populations of these places. Once everyone is standing on a sheet of newspaper, the teacher will tap members of the class on the shoulder asking:

■ What can you see?

■ What can you hear?

■ What can you smell?

■ What can you taste?

■ What can you touch?

Some examples for the children might be: 'I can taste the stale bread they give us to eat', 'I can see more poor people coming in' or 'I can smell the sweat of everyone working'. When there are a number of replies, the teacher can ask the group to start walking again, before calling out another location. As the children begin to walk around again, teacher takes away a few sheets of newspaper before calling out the next location. In this way, each time the children need to find a sheet of newspaper to stand on, they have fewer choices and become more tightly packed. Finally, as the children walk around the room, the teacher will call out 'freeze' and this time, when the teacher taps members of the class on the shoulder, they can use their favourite example of a sense from any location, for example: 'I can hear the baby crying', 'I can hear the men coming out of the brewery', 'I can smell the candles in the church' or 'I can see the beer being poured'. The teacher will then ask everyone to speak their example out loud all together, repeating the phrase over and over creating a cacophony, loud and oppressive, such as the one Dr John Snow encountered in 1854.

Further background information

In the summer of 1854, the most terrible outbreak of cholera occurred in Soho, London. In the space of just a few days well over one hundred people died. Dr John Snow, a resident of Soho, was able to trace the source of the outbreak to a water pump on Broad Street, which had been contaminated by sewage. He used a map to plot where the deaths were occurring and by making careful enquiries among the local population he was led to the place where many of the victims collected their water. Eventually, he was able to persuade the authorities to remove the handle of the pump and take it out of use. This would have needed good evidence as at the time it was believed that cholera was caused by 'bad air'. There were also interesting aspects to the epidemic, for example inmates of the local workhouse seemed to suffer very little in the outbreak, as did employees of the local brewery. This seemed to be explained by the fact that the workhouse had its own water well and the brewery workers were given an allowance of beer to drink and so were much less likely to drink the water from the pump. Dr John Snow is recognised as a founding father of 'epidemiology', the study of how often different groups of people might be affected by disease and why this is.

Follow on activity

Now that the class are becoming familiar with the atmosphere of the locality in which John Snow worked, they can be gathered back together to continue their explorations of the cholera outbreak and its source.

For this exercise, the teacher prepares a number of cards or strips of paper, preferably one for each child, which they will choose at random as they sit in a circle. On each card or strip, there will be the title of a character suggested by the locations that they have explored. There will also be an indication of an activity or action that the character is involved in and in addition some of the character strips will also be marked with an 'X', which will become important later in the exercise. The character strips can be written as follows:

1. 'I am a child carrying my pail to the water pump.' X

2. 'I am the local vicar visiting a very sick person on this street.'

3. 'I am a mother nursing my sick baby.' X

4. 'I live on this street; I'm queuing up for water at the pump.' X

5. 'I work at the brewery; I'm loading the heavy barrels.'

6. 'I'm in the church praying for my sick brother.'

7. 'I live on this street; I'm washing my front step.' X

8. 'I'm in charge of the workhouse; I make sure everyone works hard.'

9. 'I live in the workhouse; I'm too hungry to work.'

10. 'I'm taking water from the pump to my neighbour, they are too sick to come. 'X

11. 'I'm delivering barley to the brewery in my cart.'

12. 'I'm a stranger, I'm lost; I need to ask directions.'

13. 'I'm visiting my sister who is sick; I've walked a long way and I'm thirsty.' X

14. 'I work in the office at the brewery; it's a very hot day.'

15. 'I'm in a hurry, so I'm pushing in the queue at the water pump.' X

16. 'I'm arguing with someone who has pushed in the queue at the water pump.' X

17. 'I have to walk along here to get to work; I can't stand the smell of the street.'

18. 'I collect money for charity; I'm going to see the brewery owner.'

19. 'I'm in my house, washing my children's faces.' X

20. 'I arrived at the workhouse today; I've been separated from my family.'

21. 'I am carrying water home to my mother, it's so heavy and I keep spilling it.' X

22. 'I am counting the barrels of beer at the brewery.'

23. 'I am collecting water to cool my sick children at home.' X

24. 'I have come to visit my friend whose husband has died.'

25. 'I have decided to leave this street and move somewhere else.'

26. 'I don't live round here, but I come for water, it tastes better from this pump.' X

27. 'There's a hole in my water bucket, it's all running out!' X

28. 'I'm the cleaner at the church, washing the floors.'

29. 'I'm borrowing money from my friend to pay for a doctor for my child.'

30. 'I'm lending money to my friend to pay for a doctor, but I'm poor myself.'

Once all the cards have been given out, the teacher will then invite the children, one by one in turn, to step inside the circle and read out what it says on their strip of paper. When they have done this, they will take up a still and 'frozen' position to show what their character is doing or perhaps feeling. In this way, we will build up a whole class tableau. As the children gradually recognise characters doing similar things to themselves, they may choose to go and stand or sit near them, making little groups in the tableau. Once everyone has taken up a 'frozen' position to show their character, the teacher reveals one last character strip; it says: 'I am a doctor called John Snow; I am visiting this street today.' The teacher tells the class that they will be Dr Snow and perhaps has an item or prop to show that they are a doctor. Putting this item down for a moment and as the teacher again, they explain that when they clap their hands, the scene will come to life for ten seconds, so that the characters, including themselves, can move around and speak to each other if they wish. At the end of ten seconds, the teacher claps their hands again to stop the action.

Next, the teacher will ask anyone who found an 'X' on their character strip to step out of the circle and sit at the side. They will explain that all of these characters on the outside have unfortunately died from a mysterious illness that is affecting people in this part of Soho in London. The teacher will then take on the character of Dr Snow again and explain that they would like to 'interview' the characters who are left in the circle, asking them if they can remember what the other characters were doing or what they might have in common. When a few answers have been given, the teacher can come out of character and a full class discussion can begin to put together the ideas of why certain people were affected by the illness. They may discover, as John Snow did, that the source of contamination was the water pump and the people who relied on it for their water supply were at risk of becoming seriously ill. At the end of the discussion the teacher can take up the character of John Snow again, to explain in character what happened. Their speech may begin:

I am Dr John Snow and my investigations led me to discover . . .

This speech may also include some explanation about the workhouse having its own different water supply and the brewery workers being able to drink beer instead. We should also learn that Dr Snow succeeded in having the handle taken off the pump.

There is also an opportunity for a short 'mini historical play' as Dr Snow speaks to the authorities who were the Board of Guardians of the St. James Parish to persuade them that they should take the pump out of use. The children could be asked to consider, what might Dr Snow say to convince them?

APPENDIX

20

Monologue: Charting illness

Florence Nightingale

A lady dressed in a white cap and apron is counting scrubbing brushes packed in a crate.

Two hundred and ninety-seven, two hundred and ninety-eight, two hundred and ninety-nine, three hundred! Three hundred scrubbing brushes all here and what a relief that is; I was beginning to think that they would never arrive. Although, to be truthful, when I first arrived here at the hospital, I would have been glad to have had even one scrubbing brush.

Of course, I had been warned before we set out for Turkey how bad things were here. I was warned by the government and I had also read the newspaper reports that were starting to come back from the war, but I was not put off.

However, nothing could have prepared me for the horror that I and my nurses found in this army hospital. Miles of injured soldiers laid out on filthy floors, no proper sheets, just dirty rags, no proper food or clean water. The smell of the place would have made a person weaker than myself faint. Straight away I got ready to face the enemy, and I don't mean the Russian army. I mean our chief enemy: dirt and disease. It seems astonishing but cholera, typhoid, and dysentery had killed more of our men in this very hospital than the war itself. Still, I have my own weapons to fight with: soap, water and decent food.

Those of us here can see the difference that it makes to saving lives when the hospital itself is clean and decent. The difficulty is how to prove it to the people far away in England. If I can only prove to the people in charge that we must have better hospitals, then I will do the most good. I must make myself so clear that they cannot fail to see that I am right. So, I am keeping a careful record of every death here and how it was caused, whether it was from injuries on the battlefield or disease. I have made a circular chart and I have coloured

227

the deaths from the battlefield in red and deaths from disease in blue. Well, it is clear, perfectly obvious: the large area of blue when we first arrived and so much less blue after my ways of nursing had been used. We are still losing men from disease but not as many as before, the diagram shows this clearly. We can and we must improve our army hospitals, we must monitor what is needed to make them cleaner and better; we owe it to our brave soldiers.

I and my nurses are kept very busy here and I will tell you something, I can tell straight away if a girl is going to be useful to me as a nurse. I ask them: 'Are you strong?' If they are not, how can they possibly help others? I need girls who are dedicated, there is no room for a husband or children, I myself would not be able to marry and carry on my work, too. But, there is something else that a nurse needs: that is, how to give comfort. A kind word and a warm smile can make all the difference to recovering. It gives the patients hope and the strength to get better. Of course, it is not always easy, I have disagreements with the doctors, but other people's opinions don't really matter, when you know what is right.

Now, I must start my rounds. I keep my own special supply of matches for my own lamp. There is a boy, he cannot be more than nineteen, lying in a bed just along here. He was telling me about his mother and his brothers on their farm. I shall do my best to make sure that he sees them all again.

References and further reading

Agogi, E. and Stylianidou, F. (2012) Report on first survey of school practice. Creative little scientists: Enabling creativity through science and mathematics in preschool and first years of primary education. Available at: http://www.creative-little-scientists.eu/sites/default/files/D3.3_Report_on_First_Survey_of_School_Practice_FINAL.pdf. Accessed 27.1.14.

Alexander, R. (2004) *Towards Dialogic Teaching: Rethinking Classroom Talk.* 2nd Edition. Cambridge: Dialogos.

Alexander, R. (2010) *Children, Their World, Their Education. Final Report and Recommendations of the Cambridge Primary Review.* London: Routledge.

Alexander, R. J. and Flutter, J. (2009) *Towards a New Primary Curriculum: A Report from the Cambridge Primary Review. Part 1: Past and Present.* Cambridge: University of Cambridge Faculty of Education.

Assessment Reform Group (1999) *Assessment for Learning: Beyond the Black Box.* London: Nuffield Foundation.

Aubusson, P. J. and Fogwill, S. (2006) Role play as analogical modeling in science. In P. J. Aubusson, A. G. Harrison and S. M. Richie. (eds) *Metaphor and Analogy in Science Education.* Dordrecht, Netherlands: Springer.

BBC (2014) Scientists and discoveries. Available at: http://www.bbc.co.uk/education/topics/zw44j. Accessed 23.7.14

Black, P. and Wiliam, D. (1998). *Inside the Black Box.* London: nferNelson.

Black, P., Harrison, C., Lee, C., Marshall, B. and Wiliam, D. (2003) *Assessment for Learning: Putting it into Practice.* Maidenhead: Open University Press.

Blank, A. (2008) Where has the third core subject gone? *Primary Science* 105: 4–6.

Bransford, J. and Donovan, M. S. (2005) Scientific inquiry and how people learn. In Donovan, M. S. and Bransford, J. (eds) *How Students Learn: History, Mathematics and Science in the Classroom.* Washington, DC: The National Academies Press pp. 397–420.

Brodie, E. (2010) Learning science through history. *Primary Science* 111: 25–27.

Carr, M. (2001) *Assessment in the Early Childhood: Learning Stories*. London: Sage.

Clipson-Boyles, S. (2006) *Drama in Primary English Teaching*. London: David Fulton Publishers.

Collins, P. (2011) Paleontology footprint puzzle. Available at: https://sites.google.com/site/sed695b3/projects/discrepant-events/paleontology-pam-collins Accessed 23.7.14

Department for Education (2009) Assessing pupils' progress. Available at: nationalstrategies.standards.dcsf.gov.uk/node/259801. Accessed 09.03.12.

Department for Education (2012) Reporting and assessment arrangements. Available at: http://www.education.gov.uk/schools/teachingandlearning/assessment/a00197251/assessment-and-reporting-arrangements Accessed 29.2.12.

Department for Education (2013) The National Curriculum for England. Available at: www.education.gov.uk/nationalcurriculum. Accessed 1.7.13.

Dorian, K. R. (2009) Science through drama: A multiple case exploration of the characteristics of drama activities used in secondary science lessons. *International Journal of Science Education* 31 (16): 2247–2270.

Duit, R. and Treagust, D. F. (2003) Conceptual change: A powerful framework for improving science teaching and learning. *International Journal of Science Education* 25 (6): 671–688.

Guest, G. (2003) Alternative frameworks and misconceptions in primary science. University of West of England, Bristol. Available at: http://sci-tutors.gnxt.net/downloads/professional_issues/teaching/misconceptions/alternative_frameworks.pdf. Accessed 6.3.12.

Harlen, W. (2006) *Teaching, Learning and Assessing Science 5–12*. London: Sage.

Harlen, W. (2008) Science as a key component of the primary curriculum: A rationale with policy implications. Perspectives on Education 1 (Primary Science). Available at: www.wellcome.ac.uk/perspectives. Accessed 23.09.08.

Harlen, W. (2010) Principles and big ideas of science education. Hatfield: Association of Science Education Available at: www.ase.org.uk. Accessed 2.9.2011.

Harlen, W. (ed) (2011) *ASE Guide to Primary Science Education*. Hatfield: Association of Science Education.

Harlen, W. (ed) (2012) *ASE Guide to Primary Science Education*. Hatfield: Association of Science Education.

Harrison, C. and Howard, S. (2009) *Inside the Primary Black Box*. London: GL Assessment.

Harrison, C. and Howard, S. (2010) Issues in primary assessment 1: Assessment purposes. *Primary Science* 115: 5–7.

Harrison, C. and Howard, S. (2011) Issues in primary assessment 2: Assessment for learning: How and why it works in primary classrooms. *Primary Science* 116: 5–7.

Lipman, M. (2003) *Thinking in Education. 2nd Edition*. Cambridge: Cambridge University Press

Manchester Evening News (2007) City Kids think cows lay eggs. Available at: http://www.manchestereveningnews.co.uk/news/local-news/city-kids-think-cows-lay-981286 Accessed 23.7.14

Martinovic, D., Wiebe, N., Ratkovic, S., Willard-Holt, C., Spencer, T. and Cantalini-Williams, M. (2012) 'Doing research was inspiring': Building a research community with teachers. *Educational Action Research* 20 (3): 385–406.

McGregor, D. (2007) *Developing Thinking; Developing Learning. A Thinking Skills Guide for Education.* Maidenhead: Open University Press.

McGregor, D. (2010) Dramatic science: Supporting children becoming more dramatic in learning science. Bristol: Report to Astra Zeneca Science Teachers Trust.

McGregor, D. (2011) Dramatic science: Using historical drama to enliven and inform understanding about how science works at KS 2. Bristol: Report to Astra Zeneca Science Teachers Trust.

McGregor, D. (2012a) Dramatic science: Consolidating dramatic approaches to teaching science to ensure inclusivity. Bristol: Report to Astra Zeneca Science Teachers Trust.

McGregor, D. (2012b) Dramatising science learning: Findings from a pilot study to re-invigorate elementary science pedagogy for five- to seven-year olds. *International Journal of Science Education* 34 (8): 1145–1165.

McGregor, D. and Precious, W. (2010) Applying dramatic science to develop process skills. *Science and Children* 48 (2): 56–59

McGregor, D. and Precious, W. (2012) Dramatic science at Key Stage 1: Modelling ideas within an Olympics theme. *Primary Science* 123: 10–13

McSharry, G. and Jones, S. (2000) Role play in science teaching and learning. *School Science Review* 82 (298): 73–82.

Murphy, C. and Beggs, J. (2003) Children's attitudes toward school science. *School Science Review* 84 (308): 109–116.

Neelands, J. (2002) *Making Sense of Drama: A Guide to Classroom Practice.* Oxford: Heinemann.

Ofsted (2005) Removing barriers: A can-do attitude. Available at: www.Ofsted.gov.uk. Accessed 24.4.10.

Ofsted (2008) Learning outside the classroom. Available at: www.Ofsted.gov.uk. Accessed 24.4.10.

Ofsted (2011) Successful science: An evaluation of science education in England 2007–2010. Available at: www.Ofsted.gov.uk. Accessed 15.2.11.

Ofsted (2013) Maintaining curiosity. A survey into science education in schools. Available at: http://www.ofsted.gov.uk/resources/maintaining-curiosity-survey-science-education-schools. Accessed 21.7.14.

Pollard, A., Triggs, P., Broadfoot, P., McNess, E. and Osborn, M. (2000) *What Pupils Say: Changing Policy and Practice in Primary Education.* London: Continuum.

Primary Science Teaching Trust (2014) Available at: http://www.pstt.org.uk. Accessed 23.7.14.

Reay, D. and Wiliam, D. (1999) 'I'll be a nothing': Structure, agency and the construction of identity through assessment. *British Educational Research Journal* 25: 343–354.

Rose, J. (2008) *Independent review of the primary curriculum.* Available at: www.dcsf.gov. uk/primarycurriculumreview. Accessed 10.3.09.

Varelas, M., Pappas, C. C, Tucker-Raymond, E., Kane, J., Hankes, J., Ortiz, I. and Keblawe-Shamah, N. (2010) Drama activities as ideational resources for primary-grade children in urban science classrooms. *Journal of Research in Science Teaching* 47 (3): 302–325.

Wiliam, D. (2011) *Embedded Formative Assessment.* Bloomington, IN: Solution Tree Press.

Williams, J. D. (2002) Ideas and evidence in science: The portrayal of scientists in GCSE textbooks. *School Science Review* 84 (307): 89–101.

Yoon, H. G. (2006) The nature of science drama in science education. Available at: http://sciencedrama.cnue.ac.kr/admin/upload/non/yoon(2006).pdf. Accessed 5.8.2012.

Index

Introductory Note

When the text is within a table, the number span is in *italic*.

When the text is within a figure, the number span is in **bold**.

When the text is a teaching monologue (appendices), the number span is <u>underlined</u>.